MARSHA G. SPRADLIN

BROADMAN PRESS
NASHVILLE, TENNESSEE

© Copyright 1991 • Broadman Press
All Rights Reserved
4250-95
ISBN: 0-8054-5095-5
Dewey Decimal Classification: 248.3
Subject Headings: PRAYER // MEDITATION
Library of Congress Catalog Number: 90-23498
Printed in the United States of America

Unless otherwise noted, all Scripture quotations are taken from the Holy Bible, *New International Version*, copyright © 1973, 1978, 1984 by International Bible Society.

All Scripture quotations marked (KJV) are from the *King James Version* of the Bible.

All Scripture quotations marked (TLB) are from *The Living Bible*. Copyright © Tyndale House Publishers, Wheaton, Illinois, 1971. Used by permission.

Library of Congress Cataloging-in-Publication Data

Spradlin, Marsha G., 1954-
   With love, Marsha / Marsha G. Spradlin.
      p.   cm.
   ISBN 0-8054-5095-5
   1. Bible—Meditations.   2. Prayers   I. Title.
BS483.5.S67 1991
242—dc20   90-23498
                                                                                   CIP

To the children in my life

Chris
While you may only be eighteen,
your sensitivity to the Father is my inspiration.

Rachael
You are amazing. At only sixteen,
your creativity and beauty emulate the Father.

Brooke
You're finally fourteen. Your enthusiasm is
a testimony of your love of life.

Paige
You're only ten, but already you have
captured the hearts of all who know you.

Justin
You are a miracle. Only seven years ago we wondered
if you would live. Your happy life is evidence
of God's majesty and miracle.

Sean
Your six years have been painful ones for all of us.
Like your brother, Justin, your pain turned into our gain.
Your life is evidence of love.

My prayer for you is simple.
May you never lose your innocence. May you always seek
the Father's face. May you always remember what your parents
have taught you. In Jesus' Name.

Contents

Preface 7

PART 1: Your Magnificence 9
Your Heartbeat 11
A Time of Refreshment................................. 14
Above the Storm 17
A Secret Place 21
Of Sacred Heritage....................................... 26
In Pursuit of Solitude 29
My Father's Eyes... 32
Please . . . Pick the Roses............................. 35
The Symphony.. 39
Now Is the Only Time 42

PART 2: Your Miracles 45
A Time to Love... 47
That None Shall Be Lost 50
The Teacher 54
A Divine Intervention................................... 58
Unto Me.. 61
A Severe Joy.. 64
Two Doors Down 68
The Gardener 71
Perfect Timing 74
A Magnificent Encounter 77
The Tapestry 81

PART 3: Your Mysteries 85
The Mystery of Your Magnificence 87
The Cornerstone..................................... 91
A Time to Grow 94
Warm and Wonderfully Made 98
Going Home... 102
A Voice in the Wind 106
Who's Who?... 110
A Spring Cleaning 112
The Imitator.. 115
A Lesson for the Least of These 118
Be Thou My Vision.................................. 121
Feed My Sheep...................................... 125
Sh'h, Be Still....................................... 129

PART 4: Your Mercies............................... 133
Out of Darkness..................................... 135
Come . . . Follow Me 138
A Course in Humility 142
Make Up Your Mind 145
Teachable Moment 148
What's Your Excuse? 152
Falling Forward..................................... 156
The Gift 161
Out of Sight 164
The Resolution...................................... 167
The Search 171

Preface

Dear Father:

I stumbled through the door, dropping the mail on the floor. *Why does life have to be so complicated?* I thought. *Each day brings a new challenge that tests my faith. Will this day ever end?*

Then, Your letters caught my eye. They had been there all along. I had become so caught up in my routines that I had not recalled they were were there.

I stopped and picked them up. *There are so many. Why haven't I been reading every day?* I asked myself.

Each letter offered hope for a peaceful today and brighter tomorrow. Each seemed written with a message especially for me.

It's been years since I began faithfully reading Your letters. I am viewing insights and truths with a new light. Your letters have helped me with you have given me. They have helped me realize that my many ordinary and difficult days are simply a test of my faith.

I will read Your letters every day. It may take some time. As each letter becomes etched within my heart and mind, the more I will learn to live by Your truth. I must read every line and heed what You say deep within. Father, Your letters must become the very heart of me.

And as my eyes are touched by Your Word, I begin to see Your face on every page, as well as in the activities of my day. I sense Your overwhelming love and graciousness. Why else would You have taken such time to write especially to me? With each line I am moved to answer you with love. Your letters are becoming fires that burn deep inside me. They give me strength to survive and appreciate the seasons of my life.

Thank you for each letter. To show my love, I must make time to

8
With Love, Marsha

write You. You already know what's on my mind, but writing helps me understand myself better. As I close each letter, I use a phrase I have always taken for granted. But, now, these familiar words leap out at me as I see them written. There are two words that have now become my heart's desperate prayer. Lord, I sign my life to you with a strong and honest wish to be the very best me that I can ever be, and also as others read my life may they only see.

With love,
Marsha

PART 1:
Your Magnificence

"Who can be compared with you in majesty?" (Ezek. 31:2).

Your Heartbeat

Dear Child:
 Here is My message for you today from My Word:
 Many sat at the Lord's feet listening to what He said.
 But a wise man listens to advice.
 He who listens to you listens to me.

Your Father
(Luke 10:39; Prov. 12:15; Luke 10:16)

12
With Love, Marsha

Dear Father:

Summer is a beautiful time to listen. The sounds of nature are amplified by Your majesty. I hear Your voice in the sea breeze as I sit on the sandy shore. I hear Your voice as the sea gull dips into the water. I hear Your voice as the roaring tide is released from the ocean, splashing the seashore with foam and mist. I hear Your voice as children run to capture the waves and fill their buckets with sand and assorted seashells. Their laughter spills into my ears and restores my heart.

Today's experience at the beach was one of listening. I heard Your voice through Christopher, my three-year-old beach companion. To comfort my nephew after a fall, I held him close to my chest. As I gently caressed his tiny head, his tears diminished, and his rapid breathing calmed. He raised his head and said, "When you love me, I can hear your heartbeat."

This reminds me of Your love, Father. Many times, You picked me up and held me tightly. I often hear Your heartbeat and experience Your consistent love while running but, most often, after falling down.

Would I know the depth of Your love if I had never fallen? Would I take time to stop, listen, and respond? Your love does not depend on my shifts in position. It is always constant—always beating.

Perhaps pain, both physical and emotional, is an opportunity to check my relationship to You. Pain can be like a two-edged sword. It can cut or serve me. I can draw close and allow You to wrap Your arms tightly around me and teach me Your way. Or, I can become destructive, bitter, and independent, asking questions like "Why me, Father!"

Why else do so many believers attribute their most profound spiritual growth to times of pain? During painful situations, we automatically run to You for help. We find ourselves in a position to listen.

My running to You, as well as my listening to You, comes in many forms. I listen as I read Your letters and place myself at the feet of the inspired writers who unfold Your mysteries. I listen to You when I pray. Prayer becomes my lifeline, my source, and my way to recover and discover You, as well as myself. I listen to You when I write You letters. As I go back and reread each one, I can trace Your hand in my life. Writing to You each day helps me come to grips with an enormous part of my inner person about which I have never been fully honest.

13
Your Heartbeat

Writing is listening. No longer do my fears and struggles remain inside. They are surfaced and confronted as I hear You whisper.

Listening, regardless of the method, clarifies my position with You, clears my perspective, calms me toward a communion of Your spirit with my spirit as I separate my destructive ambition from Your genuine call, and challenges me to act in response to what You have said.

But, Father, is it necessary to wait for pain to know Your love? Certainly not. It is better to draw close to You daily. Only when I come persistently to You as a listener can I fully hear and appreciate the consistency of Your heartbeat.

Father, teach me to listen to Your still small voice. As I perceive Your divine whisper, transform my life to become sincerely Yours.

With love,
Marsha

A Time of Refreshment

Dear Child:

He is like a tree planted by streams of water, which yields its fruit in season and whose leaf does not wither. Whatever he does prospers.

He makes me lie down in green pastures, he leads me beside quiet waters, he restores my soul.

Each man will be like a shelter from the wind and a refuge from the storm, like streams of water in the desert and the shadow of a great rock in a thirsty land.

They will neither hunger nor thirst, nor will the desert heat or the sun beat upon them. He who has compassion on them will guide them and lead them beside springs of water.

The Lord will guide you always; he will satisfy your needs in a sun-scorched land and will strengthen your frame. You will be like a well-watered garden, like a spring whose water never fails.

I will lead them beside streams of water on a level path where they will not stumble.

If you knew the gift of God and who it is that ask you for a drink, you would have asked him and he would have given you living water.

Let us draw near to God with a sincere heart in full assurance of faith, having our hearts sprinkled to cleanse us from a guilty conscience and having our bodies washed with pure water.

Your Father
(Pss. 1:3, 23:2-3; Isa. 32:2; 49:10; 58:11; Jer. 31:9; John 4:10; Heb. 10:22)

15
A Time of Refreshment

Dear Father:

As I sit on the edge of a rushing brook, my toes beneath the icy stream's surface, I feel Your refreshing Spirit. The sounds of the wind mingling through the leaves serve me well. My mind is relaxed. The sights of the whirlpool rushing and water swirling over the sharply shaped stones, strangely enough, present a picture of peace. The velvet-like touch of the green moss tightly glued to the cold rocks supporting my back reminds me of Your support in troubled times.

This setting gives me fresh insight into how You have used nature to serve You. I see it in the words of Your letter. I feel it as I let the air breathe for me. I sense Your Spirit.

You often have used *water* to describe Your love and care for me. I realize the word is symbolic, but it is a perfect description. I can survive without food longer than I can without water. It is essential to life.

Just thinking about a tall, cool glass of water makes me want to drink. You have engineered my body to know when I need a drink. My brain has a tiny nerve center that alerts me. When my cells and blood contain enough water, I have "water-balance"—the right amount for my body to maintain health. The right balance is essential since my body is 50 to 70 percent water.

Water is vital, even though it is not digested or burned for energy. Your living water is absolutely essential for my spiritual growth. Like natural water, it must always be present. Unlike food which I can store for future use, spiritual water must continue to flow.

The presence of natural water in my body serves as my system's natural lubricant. Water helps my joints move smoothly and even allows my eyes to swivel freely. When I am dehydrated, my eyes notice first. They become irritated and dry.

The presence of Your *spiritual* water in my life serves as a spiritual lubricant. It helps my spirit move freely, even during difficult times. When I lack the power of Your Spirit, my spiritual sight is the first to notice. I begin to lose perspective.

My healthy body has no difficulty maintaining a water balance. A water loss of as little as 1 percent makes me thirsty. But if I wait for thirst to signal the need for natural water, my body is somewhat depleted. Likewise, a spiritual imbalance—the slight loss of time with You—can cause my soul to thirst. But waiting for spiritual thirst to signal the

16
With Love, Marsha

need for Your living water means my spirit is already somewhat depleted.

When I am healthy, it is difficult for me to drink too much water. Likewise, I can never imbibe too much of Your living water. When I am thirsty I must drink. But, when I am not thirsty, I must also drink from Your streams of living water. When I let my body become a channel for Your living water, others will truly know that I am Yours.

With love,
Marsha

Above the Storm

Dear Child:

Do you not know? Have you not heard? The Lord is the everlasting God, the Creator of the ends of the earth. He will not grow tired or weary, and his understanding no one can fathom. He gives strength to the weary and increases the power of the weak. Even youths grow tired and weary, and young men stumble and fall; but those who hope in the Lord will renew their strength. They will soar on wings like eagles; they will run and not grow weary, they will walk and not be faint.

Your Father
(Isa. 40:28-31)

18
With Love, Marsha

Dear Father:

Your letter today touched my heart. The timing was perfect. You brought the eagle to my attention. I really had not thought much about the eagle before today. In fact, I am not certain I have seen a real eagle except at the zoo. To understand Your message completely, I pulled out the encyclopedia and a few bird books. I was amazed to discover why You chose the eagle to teach me about freedom to soar.

Soaring is the act of flying upward. The eagle is the symbol of soaring as well as commitment to excellence. For thousands of years, the eagle has been revered and esteemed. No doubt, one reason the eagle is so respected is its ability to soar with grandeur and grace in flight.

The eagle symbolizes power and freedom. It is admired for its great size and awesome freedom. It was the official symbol of the Romans, Charlemagne, and Napoleon and has been on the official seal of the United States since 1782. What are the characteristics of one who soars?

Grandeur. The eagle is large; it has a seven-foot wingspan and is thirty to thirty-five inches tall. It is one of the largest, most powerful birds in the world with a life span of twenty to twenty-five years. Father, so often I feel intimidated. Help me to recognize my own grandeur, my potential because of You in my life.

Speed. While the eagle may appear slow because of size, it has been observed flying across a two-mile lake in one minute. That's 120 miles per hour. An eagle can soar to heights of one-half mile and descend at the rate of 200 miles per hour. Father, how fast am I to recognize needs and respond? Teach me to soar.

Power. The eagle can actually carry objects equal to its own weight, about twelve pounds. Father, I can only become a powerful witness as I recognize You as my source of power. Teach me to carry a load equal to the power and potential You have given to me. Teach me to remember that You are my refuge and strength—a fortress. Help me to realize the powerful influence I can have in the world.

Vision. The eagle can see with his eyes shut. In addition to its normal pair of eyelids, the eagle has a set of clear eyelids called membranes. The membranes can be closed for protection from wind and hungry eaglets without affecting the eagle's vision. Father, I may need an eye examination. In order to soar, I need vision protected by Your Spirit. As I encounter various trials, may my focus remain consistent.

19
Above the Storm

How does the eagle become such an incredible bird? It learns through trial and error; it builds its nest high; it waits; and it is renewed.

An eagle starts young and learns through trial and error. After two or three months in the security of the nest, the young eaglet is ready to fly. The first flight is to a nearby branch or rock. Next, the eaglet is carried by the current of the parent eagle. During training, the parent coaxes and calls the eaglet. Father, how often am I guilty of wanting to skip the primary steps needed for spiritual growth? Teach me to listen as I am called and coaxed by You. Remind me that I am only asked to go or do in proportion to my obedience and ability to listen.

An eagle builds its nest high—usually in the mountains or cliffs. The purpose is protection. A high nest puts the eagle in a position to survey all that is below. The additional height makes an excellent and quick launching pad enabling the eagle to gain sufficient speed for its gradual climb into the sky. Teach me, Father, to build my nest high in order to secure Your protection, have Your vision, and have the ability to quickly respond with momentum and power. Building my nest high might mean setting high goals, standards, and priorities.

The eagle learns to wait. It waits for the right opportunity to fly. Sometimes it is grounded, but it doesn't give up. Father, I am often restless. I do not like to wait. Teach me that learning to soar means learning to wait. It takes time. There may be times when I am grounded. Teach me not to give up. Often the process of waiting is my training. Teach me to wait for the perfect opportunity to soar.

The eagle knows renewal. It realizes it cannot soar every moment. Each year, its feathers are replaced over a period of several months. No two adjacent feathers fall out at once; therefore, the eagle is not handicapped during the renewal period. Teach me, Father, to find time to be renewed. I must renew myself spiritually through my own quiet time, Bible study, and fellowship with other Christians. Help me not to equate this renewal time as lazy time. It is a time to grow, not a time to concentrate on my handicaps. Teach me to remain in the shadow of Your wings.

How does the eagle's soaring demonstrate commitment toward excellence? The eagle learns how to glide, take risks, and decrease in size. All are qualities of excellence.

I was amazed to learn that while soaring, the eagle really does not

20
With Love, Marsha

move its wings. Instead, it glides after takeoff. It only moves its wings to take off and accelerate. Father, if I am to soar, I must not frantically flutter and flap my wings. I relax and let You glide for me. To obtain amazing heights in my relationship with You, I must let You do the acceleration and be the perfecter of every good work in me.

The eagle is a risk taker. It flies in storms when other birds seek shelter. Help me, Father, be willing to take risks in order to rise above ground level and even over the storm. Only then can I see Your solutions to problems that so often ground me. Am I willing to risk in relationships and responsibilities? Teach me to soar through risk taking.

As the eagle soars, its size appears to decrease. Actually, it remains the same size, but from the ground, the eagle appears to become smaller. As I soar, Father, may my view of myself, needs, and wants decrease. Only when my concentration on myself decreases can I obtain a bird's-eye view of the world. Teach me to decrease in size so that You might increase within me.

Lately, I have felt like a tiny bird with a broken wing. I have been locked inside my cage. Your letter set me free. You have reached inside of me to heal the hurt. Until now, I have fled each time You reached in to comfort my pain. I have dwelled in the agonies of a mindless flight that has become more than I could bear. Like a frightened child who runs, I have wanted to trust, yet, I have only watched fearfully.

Now I realize that everything I need is here, within my heart. I can soar far above the storm on the shadow of Your wings. Such wings are spread strong and wide. No longer do I need to dash myself against the stones and feel terrified. You are here to heal my wounds and lift me above the storm. The storm may come and go, but I will hide in the shadow of Your wings. Give me wings to soar as an eagle. Teach me to walk and not grow weary. I will run and not faint. You have given me freedom to fly. As I exercise my freedom, I demonstrate confidence that I am sincerely Yours.

With love,
Marsha

A Secret Place

Dear Child:
 He will make your righteousness shine like the dawn, the justice of your cause like the noonday sun.

Your Father
(Ps.37:6)

22
With Love, Marsha

Dear Father:

The sun had just risen. Painted clearly across the sky were the brilliant shades of pink, blue, and purple. Accenting them was the reflection of the sun shimmering off the ocean waves. The familiar echoes of the waves escaping the ocean and clapping the sandy beach reminded me of many childhood vacation trips to the beach with my family. That seemed long ago and far away.

It felt bracing to let the salty air virtually breathe for me. This day was special. I wanted to celebrate. What an extraordinary place this was to start a special day. I built my sanctuary under the sun, carefully spreading my blanket near the water's edge. I unpacked Your letters, my notebook, and pen, and exulted: "Let's celebrate."

It was Labor Day weekend. As was our family custom, Mother and Daddy planned their traditional family day at Gulf Shores, Alabama. They seemed thrilled that I could take off a couple days to join them here. They must have sensed that this had been a hard year for me. The pressures of work and life had captured my every thought. I no longer felt breathing room to maintain my life, much less become what You designed for me.

While it is enjoyable to be with my family, I wanted some time all to myself. I couldn't remember the last time I was all alone with You. My days had become crowded clusters of camouflaged misery. Maybe that was why on the first morning at Gulf Shores I slipped away early. Everyone else was still in bed.

The aesthetic beauty was exactly as I had remembered it, but one thing was very different. Me! I was physically and, unfortunately, spiritually only a shadow of what I was years ago. So much had happened that could have left my body and soul battered, bruised, and abused. Yet, because of You, my body and spirit were stronger than ever. I remember what You said in Your letter: "The one who is in you is greater than the one who is in the world" (1 John 4:4).

I knew I had to hurry. It would not be long until the quiet, private beach would fill up with people, beach balls, and the smell of hamburgers and hot dogs cooking over hot coals. Yet, at this moment, there were only two of us there, You and me.

It was too hard to write with the wind blowing the pages of my notebook and pulling my thoughts toward Your beauty. I felt frustrated.

23
A Secret Place

The gentle breeze was just strong enough to tangle the pages of Your letters. I fought it, so I put my pen down.

I gathered my books and pens merely to sit on the cold sand. This allowed me to experience something entirely new. You taught me as I just listened and watched. I learned a deeper meaning of love and divine security.

Quietly, I watched in amusement as the white, foamy waves washed to shore and then quickly fled the seashore to rejoin the ocean. They left behind a form of life—tiny sea crabs. They seemed stranded and almost frightened. Their little legs hurried them back toward the ocean as if their lives depended on it. The moment they reached the ocean, they were quickly washed back to the shore by another wave of liquid motion. The cycle repeated itself in tranquil, alternating rhythm.

Those silly sea crabs, I thought. *If they would relax and only be still, a stronger wave would take them back to the ocean where they belonged.* But, no. They did not see beyond that frightening moment.

Suddenly, I felt like a sea crab. How could I have been so blind? Why had I been fighting so long? The past year of living in the fast lane had made me feel like a mighty wave was tossing me to and fro and even slapping me down at times. Just as I had felt I was making progress, I felt knocked back into the storm. *If only I could learn to rest and let You love me*, I thought. I saw that healing and rest come in waiting for the waves of pain and restlessness to reverse their flow. I wondered if the painful flow would reverse if I were to go ahead and acknowledge the presence of Your love.

The rhythmic clapping of the waves had a continual tranquil effect. I closed my eyes and chose to listen to the waves. Instead of hearing them reject the tiny crabs, I heard them rescue them. This paralleled so beautifully my own spiritual healing.

Quietly, I prayed, "Father, You have not brought me the pain and frustration of a rushing life-style. You have allowed me to experience it. You have not abandoned me. Instead, You are there each day as I rush through life, ready to receive me and my frazzled insecurities."

I closed my eyes to continue to pray and heard sounds of solitude. I felt sleepy. My mind began to float gently over the series of events of the past year. I considered how I could have reacted differently. I remembered the little crabs. Just as they had run and panicked, I, too, had run as hard as I could from what I thought was sabotaging me. Each time You spoke my name, I fled. The agonies accompanying my flight grew more than I could bear. I thought You made me feel this way. But I was the one who continued to dash myself against the stones when Your love could have healed my wounds. Like a frightened child, I ran away. I wanted to trust, but I only watched fearfully. Everything I ever longed for was waiting for me.

Softly, my heart heard You speak. Your message was not in words my ears could hear. Instead, it was a message of love that only my heart understood.

"Marsha, wait! I am love! To know Me is to know love. My love is radically different from any love you have ever known. Come, come, to the water, let Me love you! My love does not depend on who you are, what you do, or even where you are. I love you because of who I am. Come, let Me give you My gift of love," my Father called.

As the tide moved away from its shore, I felt You gently placing a gift into my hands. With a desperate heart to know You and courage to share You, I accepted Your gift of love. As I took it, I felt wrapped in it. Accepting Your love was the wisest thing I had ever done.

I spent the entire morning sitting on the beach. Soon, other people gathered, but that was OK. I still felt all alone in my sanctuary under the Son.

As the sun rose and began to warm my body and heal my outward parts, I felt the Son rising within my spirit, warming and healing my soul with Your love. He deeply touched my wounds.

Then it happened. I felt healed. Your love was so radically different from any I had ever known.

What did You teach me about love? I remembered Your love letter from 1 Corinthians 13. Yes, Father, the greatest is love. In order to make more room for love, I must get rid of all the things within that are unloving.

As I breathed in the salty air, I breathed in Your love. As I exhaled, I imagined exhaling the pain and bitterness that had collected over the years.

I prayed, "Father, in our times alone, I have come to know the quiet words of Your love. They have gently changed my heart. Even in the storm, I am safe and warm in this secret hiding place inside my heart.

25
A Secret Place

You have covered me with grace. Here I can stand while others may fall. Meet me here again. May the effects of Your Son be obvious. Not only do I want others to notice the change in my skin color but the changes in the color of my soul."

It's late evening. This *was* a day of celebration. As I write this letter in memory of the gift of love You wrapped me in today, I write . . .

With love,
Marsha

Of Sacred Heritage

Dear Child:
For you have heard my vows, O God; you have given me the heritage of those who fear your name.
Your statutes are my heritage forever; they are the joy of my heart.
Sons are a heritage from the Lord, children a reward from him.

Your Father
(Pss. 61:5; 119:111; 127:3)

27
Of Sacred Heritage

Dear Father:

Your letter today fits perfectly with today's experience of reentering my past. As I write to You, I am reminded of my heritage. I am grateful for my past. Of course, today's experience really didn't start today—but years ago.

I remember my thirteenth birthday. For me, thirteen was not an unlucky number. On that day I was gifted with one possession I had dreamed of having since my early childhood—a trunk. This was not just any trunk; it was Grandmother's trunk.

As a young girl, I often admired the old trunk tucked under a quilt and hidden in the closet. I knew the trunk had special meaning to Grandmother. On my thirteenth birthday, Grandmother kept her promise. "One day that old trunk will be yours. I will 'will' it to you," she had promised me.

Early this morning, I received a call from Grandmother who will soon celebrate her eightieth birthday. "It's time for you to get your trunk," she announced. Grandmother's declining health made it necessary for her to enter a health-care facility. Before moving, she wanted to carry out her commitment made to me over twenty years ago.

Early this morning, a friend and I grabbed one last cup of coffee and headed north for the hour and a half drive to Grandmother's. There we found the old trunk in Grandmother's empty house. Taped to the top of the sixty-eight-year-old antique were the words, "I *will* you my trunk. *Will* you have it?"

Reading her note was an emotional moment for me. I had inherited her trunk, but I still had the choice of taking it. By accepting it, I would be assuming part of her and making that sector a portion of my own.

After taking the trunk inside my house, I unlocked the rusty latches and glimpsed inside for the first time. Not only had I accepted an antique, I had received a heritage.

Inside the trunk were many treasures. Each told me something of my heritage. As I examined the many photos and family heirlooms, I was reminded of my heritage in You.

My spiritual heritage is found in Your written Word, and its truth remains sound. You *willed* that I should receive all that is Yours—those things needed for everyday life. Many of Your treasures are things You have saved for me and want to give me at precisely the right moment in my life. Grandmother did not have to die in order for me to receive her treasure chest. Yet, Jesus did! Grandmother is still alive, but so is He! One by one I removed the articles. With each article, I marveled. I found myself pulling away from the present and entering the past. As I looked at those items that made life "easy" for Grandmother, I wondered what life was like then. Her iron was heavy because it was made of (you guessed it) iron, and her homemade clothing was simple. Each piece was made from fabric woven at home. I imagined life without an electric curling iron. I thought of traveling to church in a horse-drawn carriage. I envisioned life without the modern conveniences of microwave ovens, dishwashers, washing machines, televisions, telephones, and, most importantly, my computer.

My life-style is different from that of Grandmother, but one matter is the same: the internal and eternal resources given us through Your heritage.

The exciting reality is that I do not have to wait to receive Your many gifts. As Your child, You have instantly gifted me with all that is Yours. They are the fruit of the Spirit. I have inherited "love, joy, peace, patience, kindness, goodness, faithfulness, gentleness, and self-control. Against such things there is no law. Those who belong to Christ Jesus have crucified the sinful nature with its passions and desires. Since we live by the Spirit, let us keep in step with the Spirit" (Gal. 5:22-25).

Yes, Father, my life-style is different from Grandmother's. But my purpose and heritage in You remain the same. You made a difference in her life. Likewise, You have made a difference in mine. May I continue to discover all that is mine through You. May my life reflect my gratitude for my heritage in You. All that is Yours is mine. May all that is mine be forever Yours.

With love,
Marsha

In Pursuit of Solitude

Dear Child:
  My Presence will go with you, and I will give you rest.
  My soul finds rest in God alone: my salvation comes from him.
  In repentance and rest is your salvation, in quietness and trust is your strength.
  My people will live in peaceful dwelling places, in secure homes, in undisturbed places of rest.
  Ask where the good way is, and walk in it, and you will find rest for your souls.
  Come to me, all you who are weary and burdened, and I will give you rest. Take my yoke upon you and learn from me, for I am gentle and humble in heart, and you will find rest for your souls.
  For anyone who enters God's rest also rests from his own work, just as God did from His. Let us, therefore, make every effort to enter that rest, so that no one will fall by following their example of disobedience.
  They will rest from their labor, for their deeds will follow them.

Your Father
(Ex. 33:14; Ps.62:1; Isa. 30:15; 32:18; Jer. 6:16; Matt. 11:28-29; Heb. 4:10-11; Rev. 14:13)

30
With Love, Marsha

Dear Father:

When I stop long enough to think about rest, I remember *Alice's Adventures in Wonderland*:

" 'Will you walk a little faster?' said a whiting to a snail,
'There's a porpoise close behind us, and he's treading on my tail.' "

Father, the rush and routine of my daily life does not seem to be much different from Alice's. I do not seem to find time to yield to my natural instinct to rest.

But I am not alone. This has been called a tired generation. My friends and I view rest as a luxury—leisure. And any attempt to seize time from work for the luxury of leisure is breaking away from the workaholic mind-set and life-style that seems to be so valued in our society. No matter how hard I work, though, someone in my competitive world is willing to put in a few more hours. I simply cannot keep up with them—or myself!

My heart tells me that without a block of time to rest, I am prone to burnout and breakdown. Yet, my mind won't stop, and my ears refuse to listen. I feel I could easily go under anytime. What is all this work for, anyway? When did I get so busy that I started losing my grip and perspective on the meaning of the life You have so richly given me? Father, I have become restless. I lack a quiet and inner solitude.

Your letters speak clearly about finding rest and peace in You. I shouldn't rest just because my work is done; You have commanded me to rest because You created me to need it. After all, You rested on the first sabbath.

In six days, You created the heaven and the earth, but on the seventh day, You stopped laboring. Did You need rest? Of course not! But You chose to rest to set a precedent. By resting, You put into motion the rhythm of rest. Rest, then, is a cessation from routine. You did not intend it to be a reward or even a luxury, but a necessity.

From Your letters I am realizing that rest is a positive force. It yields security and serenity. Rest is a gift from You. It comes as I choose to be alone with You, the only One who knows the pain of my fatigue and the only source of refreshment.

Rest is the calm in the midst of the rushing winds of my own personal winter storms. It is the quietness and confidence that I experience as I

In Pursuit of Solitude

realize *Your* world is not a competitive one. Rest is the antithesis of loneliness.

Rest may mean silence. During moments of quietness and solitude, I become at one with myself and You. I gain the momentum to fly into the storm, rather than be devastated by it. I gain the momentum to be one who is able to give rather than need support.

Rest has side effects. As I spend time with You, I recognize Your magnificence. Likewise, I recognize my own magnificence. I learn to accept myself as a unique creation. I learn to enjoy myself and gain insight into how I can contribute to the quality of life for others. Only through rest do I regain meaning and maintain perspective.

Father, lead me in experiencing Your sabbath rest. May it become as needed and natural as my breathing. Because in rest I demonstrate Your calm within—a calm, secure, gentle spirit that can demonstrate to the world that I am Your child.

With love,
Marsha

My Father's Eyes

Dear Child:
   If you believe, you will receive whatever you ask for in prayer.
   We believe and know that you are the Holy One of God.
   Believe me when I say that I am in the Father and the Father is in me; or at least believe on the evidence of the miracles themselves.
   For it is with your heart that you believe and are justified, and it is with your mouth that you confess and are saved.

Your Father
(Matt. 21:22; John 6:69; 14:11; Rom. 10:10)

33
My Father's Eyes

Dear Father:

Is seeing believing? Or is believing seeing? The two seem to be so tightly woven into the fabric of potential in You that it is hard to separate the threads. I have always felt that seeing was believing. Yet, I am starting to realize that believing is seeing.

Often, I do not know where You are leading me. Yet, I do know that You are going with me. My responsibility is this: to listen to Your voice. There are times when I cannot hear it, Father, because of outside noise. If I am not hearing messages from Yourself about who I am and where I am going, then I am hearing messages from others. Sometimes these messages sound like Your voice. At other times, I am quick to recognize they are not from You. It is important that all messages be filtered through You. Any message, if heard consistently and believed, can become real to my emotions.

I once heard a story of an Indian who found an eagle's egg and put it into the nest of a prairie chicken. The eaglet hatched with the brood of chicks and grew up with them, thinking he was a chicken. He never realized he could fly. One day he saw a stately bird far above him in the cloudless sky, soaring gracefully on the powerful wind current. The tragedy of the story is that the bird never knew that he, too, was an eagle. He was convinced that he could never soar. The eagle died thinking he was only a prairie chicken.

What a tragedy! Many Christians are living examples of a similar disaster. I, too, have failed at times to recognize my potential. As impoverished Christians, we give up the desire to be the best for You. To fulfill my potential in You, I must give up such limited thinking and identify truly who I am, as well as Whose I am. Otherwise, I become disguised because of what I tell myself. I can become a victim of messages from sources other than the Source of true identity. When I do, I give up my beneficial pursuit to become all that You have created me to be.

Yes, Father, I have found myself in a situation like the eagle, even though I am aware that Your design for my life is to become all that You have designed. I know that only through Your power I can! But, I still, on occasion, set self-imposed limitations. It is much easier to think of reasons why I cannot than to venture on the pursuit for winning results.

34
With Love, Marsha

Thinking of reasons for my lack and limitation is the "chicken" way out. It takes a 180-degree turn from my current path of thinking and doing to soar with the eagles as Your winner dedicated to making my life count.

I am the only one who holds the set of keys available to unlock my doors of potential. Letting another person's perception of who I am become more important than my own simply gives the keys to others and slams the prison doors shut in my face.

Unfortunately, my perception of myself has been shaped more from the outside than the inside. Other people have told me all of my life who I am, what to do, and how to feel. Eventually, I believe that in order to be loved and accepted, I must be these things. This sets in motion the cycles of trying to live up to others's expectations. I easily become a prisoner of what other people believe.

Father, I do not have to be a victim of other people's assumptions. And, I do not have to be a prisoner of my own potential. How I imagine and perceive my world to be is how I will live in it. Therefore, it is imperative that my perception or view of my world match Yours.

Give me Your eyes, Father. Allow me to see myself as You see me. Teach me to live up to Your expectations and dreams for me, rather than the expectations of others. I am convinced that if I do not stand for something, I am vulnerable to fall for anything. Grant me strength to stand for You at all cost.

Yes, Father, believing is seeing. I believe You see me as a child that has a desperate heart to be all You want me to be.

With love,
Marsha

Please . . . Pick the Roses

Dear Child:
 The kingdom of God . . . is like a mustard seed, which is the smallest seed you plant in the ground. Yet when planted, it grows and becomes the largest of all garden plants, with such big branches that the birds of the air can perch in its shade.
 If some of the branches have been broken off, and you, though a wild olive shoot, have been grafted in among the others and now share in the nourishing sap from the olive root, do not boast over those branches. If you do, consider this: You do not support the root, but the root supports you.

Your Father
(Mark 4:30-31; Rom. 13:11-18)

36
With Love, Marsha

Dear Father:

It must be spring! I could not keep from noticing each symptom as I walked outside today. Bursting forth with scarlet color and releasing the familiar aroma were rows of rose bushes that wrapped around my house. The scarlet flowers reminded me of the rose garden in front of my childhood home. For a moment, the smell of the familiar flower created nostalgia. I found my memories returning to my own front yard. Even though I was just a child, I had an appreciation for Your creation, the rose. But this appreciation did not just happen—it grew.

Our garden of roses was an aesthetic experience for many onlookers. For most of my childhood, they were simply flowers in front of our house. They were everyday, common, trite, and merely there. Then, one day, it all changed.

I was young when I first noticed them. Well, actually, it wasn't the roses I noticed. Instead, the lack of rose bushes caught my attention. At that moment, I grieved. They must have been more special than I had realized.

I often picked them on the way to school or right before greeting Mother after a school day. They were a symbol of love. I enjoyed the hugs and smiles I received in return for this delicate creation. Since we had so many roses, I had many opportunities to be hugged.

But one day they were all practically gone. No beautiful roses, only thorny clusters enveloping our lawn. I was embarrassed to live in the house that was identified with the ugly shrubs. I felt sure every child walking past my house was bursting into laughter. We were the laughingstock of our entire neighborhood, I was sure. I felt humiliated.

"Who would do such a thing?" I cried out.

I had hardly said it when I saw him—my daddy! No one loved the rose garden more than he, yet there he stood, sort of scrunched over with a large scissor-like weapon in his hands. Snip, snip, snip; the beautiful greenery fell to the ground. As each branch was detached from its vine, I felt my ability to share my love cut out of me.

"Dad, stop! Please don't cut the flowers. What are you doing?" I asked.

"Hi, Honey! How was school?" he replied.

"What are you doing to our roses?" I asked again.

37
Please . . . Pick the Roses

"Yeah, it does look pretty funny right now, but wait a few weeks. Our roses will be more beautiful than ever," he explained.

Fortunately for me, Daddy proceeded to unravel this mystery. I soon realized that every great experience in life is really a mystery. He called this one *pruning*.

"Pruning? It looks like you're cutting down the bushes!" I said.

"Oh no. Pruning is a skill. You have to know what you're doing to prune. You see, to prune means to reduce by eliminating superficial matter," he told me.

"What?" I asked.

Daddy laughed, "Let me put explain it this way. It means to cut off or cut back parts for better shape or more fruitful growth. It means to cut away the parts you do not want, those parts that are unnecessary."

"But, why, Dad?" I asked.

"You have to get rid of what you don't need to make room for what you want," he answered.

My daddy was wise and right. In a few months the thorny bushes were more gorgeous than ever. By cutting back the excess parts, the nutrients could concentrate on certain areas of the plant. This resulted in:

- faster growth,
- a healthier plant,
- a more beautiful plant,
- a lawn that was noticed by others, and
- a greater appreciation of its beauty.

Before long, our rose garden was the talk of the neighborhood. Strangers would knock on our door to ask, "How does your garden grow so beautiful?" Maybe the reason for the attention was Daddy's sign, "Please pick the flowers!"

As an adult, I have compared this pruning experience to many of the mysteries of my own life. Often the pain of life feels like something is snipping at me. I have to remember that the experience can cut me or serve me. I choose.

You, Father, do not choose to cut me down by ill circumstances or bad times, yet You do allow such instances to occur. This shows Your total sovereignty. Why do You allow pain to touch us? I am learning that it must be because You, even more than Daddy, love me. You

With Love, Marsha

know the benefits of pruning. After all, You are the author of all of the great mysteries of the world. You could choose to block pain from entering my life, but to do so would likewise mean alleviating the potential to grow from the experience. Difficulties often cause me not only to . . .
- gain appreciation for the things I once viewed as trite;
- focus on what I don't need to make room for what I do need;
- recognize You as the Source of help; and
- acknowledge You as the One who loves me most . . .

but difficulties also cause me to:
- grow faster as a result of the pain—pain does have a way of capturing my attention;
- become a healthier person, spiritually and emotionally; and
- develop a lovely life that emulates Your Son, Jesus Christ.

Pruning really means blooming. It depends on my perspective. It can cut me or serve me. I can decide.

Father, continue to teach me the mysteries of pruning. Lead me to recognize the marvelous mystery of pruning by sharing my growth experience. In all that I say and do, let my life be a rose garden!

With love,
Marsha

The Symphony

Dear Child:
　The Lord is my strength and my song.
　He put a new song in my mouth, a hymn of praise to our God.
　Sing to the Lord a new song: sing to the Lord, all the earth. Sing to the Lord, praise his name; proclaim his salvation day after day.
　Shout for joy, O heavens; rejoice, O earth; burst into song, O mountains!
　Speak to one another with psalms, hymns, and spiritual songs. Sing and make music in your heart to the Lord, always giving thanks to God the Father for everything, in the name of our Lord Jesus Christ.
　Even in the case of lifeless things that makes sounds, such as the flute or harp, how will anyone know what tune is being played unless there is a distinction in the notes? Again, if the trumpet does not sound a clear call, who will get ready for battle? So it is with you. Unless you speak intelligible words with your tongue, how will anyone know what you are saying? You will just be speaking into the air.

Your Father
(Ex. 15:2; Pss. 40:3; 96:1-2; Isa. 49:13; Eph. 5:19-20; 1 Cor. 14:7-9)

40
With Love, Marsha

Dear Father:

I still feel the electricity in the air as I envision the opulent concert hall. As the conductor walked to his stand, a hush fell over the crowd. All eyes were focused on him. He gazed at the musicians, then gave his signal. Suddenly the majestic beginning of the spring concert performed by our city's symphony burst into the air.

I feel that perhaps many in the audience were not as engrossed as I. I remembered the days when I had sat in the performer's chair.

Years have passed since I tore into a letter that read, "Congratulations! You have been selected to join other college musicians to perform at the state education association's meeting in our capital city. This is only one performance, but it will be a once-in-a-lifetime experience. You are expected to arrive in three weeks. You will join other musicians for a one-week marathon of nonstop rehearsal. Until then, think music!"

The day finally arrived when 100 students gathered at a college in the central part of the state. We came from various backgrounds. Our ages spanned eighteen to thirty-eight. Some students were married, some were single. Other than music, we really had little in common. In fact, we felt rather awkward together at first.

We started our first rehearsal by tuning. Nothing seemed quite as boring as tuning. I remember the frustration we experienced as we patiently waited for all 100 musicians to tune to the first clarinet. Only after we tuned could we start making music.

And we did! We practiced, practiced, and practiced even more. For seven days and nights, we did nothing but practice. Mealtimes were brief to make more time for practice. But finally, the hours of rehearsal paid off. It was time for the once-in-a-lifetime performance.

We arrived at the performance center early. Could this be the same group I had been practicing with all week? No longer were we in jeans and sweatshirts. The men wore tuxedos, and the women wore black gowns. The performance was truly once in a lifetime.

Lord, You have used so many plain-vanilla experiences in my life to teach me meaningful lessons. From that week of practice, I learned that those initial awkward feelings I sometimes have—even with my Christian friends—seem to disappear when we focus on what we have in common—You. I learned that it requires effort, concentration, and

41
The Symphony

practice to become "laborers together with God." And such labor yields music only when we tune our lives individually to You, our Conductor.

Often, instead of a majestic beginning, making music with other Christians does not come as expected. On occasion, all I can hear is one little flute. Then, a violin and an oboe join in. As our lives merge, the music is intensified, but sometimes ever so slightly. As You, our Conductor, wave Your baton with intense feeling, You direct the three of us as if there were hundreds. We continue to make majestic music until we focus on what we feel is missing. Where is the rest of the orchestra?

As our Conductor, You can skillfully work with the few of us who are willing to play our parts. It is not the music we make that has meaning; it is You, the Conductor. Regardless of the number willing to play, You can make our music glorious and focus our attention on what we can do together, rather than the awkwardness we feel because there are so few of us. We can continue to make glorious music as we tune our lives to Your life and as we practice, practice, practice!

In one of Your letters, you directed a promise to those of us willing to play. You said, "If two of you on earth agree about anything you ask for, it will be done for you by my Father in heaven" (Matt. 18:19).

The word *agree* comes from the same Greek word from which we obtain *symphony*. As I agree with others in prayer and allow You to be the Conductor, then we pray in symphony. We become a concert of prayer.

Father, may my life be a concert of prayer. May my eyes always focus on You, the Conductor. Make my life an instrument that makes sweet music to Your ears. May my music be heard by those needing to hear Your sweet song. Make my song truly Yours.

With love,
Marsha

Now Is the Only Time

Dear Child:
 Wait for the Lord; be strong and take heart and wait for the Lord.
 Be still before the Lord and wait patiently for him; do not fret when men succeed in their ways, when they carry out their wicked schemes.

Your Father
(Pss. 27:14; 37:7)

43
Now Is the Only Time

Dear Father:

It is 9:06 a.m. I am late for my speaking engagement. Instead of being at my assignment, I am just now approaching 17,000 feet above sea level. The captain has turned off the seat-belt sign and given a "we're-late" address to the crowd of impatient passengers.

So, we wait. I am observing that some are waiting more constructively than others. The moments are giving way to minutes—now over one hour has passed. Some passengers are grumpy; others, angry; some feel victimized. Some, though, are using the time creatively.

Why do we get so bent out of shape when we are delayed? After all, we should be used to it. We wait in long lines at grocery stores and drive-up bank tellers. We wait on freeways and at traffic lights. Perhaps we are waiting for a phone call or a special message.

I sometimes wonder if I spend the majority of my time waiting. If I do, maybe the question should be, How well do I wait? Do I accept delays graciously, creatively, and calmly? Or, because of my "instant" mind-set, do I dread waiting? Do I let delays ground me emotionally, spiritually, and mentally?

Waiting, like change, is one of the most predictable facets of one's life. Neither life nor any of the great truths to be learned are instant. It takes time to grow, learn, and know. A flower does not bud forth from a seed overnight nor does a tree stretch forth its limbs in a month or even a year. Is it worth the wait? Perhaps patience is its own reward.

Father, if time means nothing to You, why do I become so frustrated when I have to wait on answers? I must remember that I have all the time there is. Too often, I waste Your time as I encroach on eternity.

How often, Father, have I choked on Your letters with a yawn and hindered the time I should have spent with You by remembering other things I had to do and making excuses that insist I don't have time for You? Of course, I have time, Father. I always have time to do what I feel is important. Teach me to take time.

Waiting plays an active part in growing. Yet, waiting seems to rub against my very nature. Where there is a holding pattern, there often seems to be a vacuum. Where there is an empty space, something seems to slip in making waiting patiently and purposefully almost impossible. Nature abhors the vacuum. When anything is removed, something must fill it. I am by nature a doer. I constantly feel the pressure to make

With Love, Marsha

it happen. I can't wait! Is it possible, Father, to wait patiently while I actively participate in Your plan? Or, is waiting just passive? Is there such a factor as active waiting? Could I learn to view waiting as an opportunity to invest more energy toward my defined purpose? Can I learn to wait creatively and productively?

Reveal to me Your truth that there is no space or time between us, Father. Teach me not to think beyond the limits of my birth and death. Instead, reveal to me the importance of now! Could it be that only through waiting do I realize and appreciate the importance of the many moments of my life? Now is the only time there is. To be what you want, I must accept my responsibility to use time wisely as I wait.

With love,
Marsha

PART 2:
Your Miracles

"He came to Jesus at night and said, 'Rabbi, we know you are a teacher who has come from God. For no one could perform the miraculous signs you are doing if God were not with him' " (John 3:2).

A Time to Love

Dear Child:

One man gives freely, yet another gains even more; another withholds unduly, but comes to poverty. A generous man will prosper; he who refreshes others will himself be refreshed. People curse the man who hoards grain, but blessing crowns him who is willing to sell.

If I speak in the tongues of men and of angels, but have not love, I am only a resounding gong or a clanging cymbal. If I have the gift of prophecy and can fathom all mysteries and all knowledge, and if I have a faith that can move mountains, but have not love, I am nothing. If I give all I possess to the poor and surrender my body to the flames, but have not love, I gain nothing. Love is patient, love is kind. It does not envy, it does not boast, it is not proud. It is not rude, it is not self-seeking, it is not easily angered, it keeps no record of wrongs. Love does not delight in evil but rejoices with the truth. It always protects, always trust; always hopes, always perseveres. Love never fails.

For God did not give us a spirit of timidity, but a spirit of power, of love, and of self-discipline.

There is no fear in love. But perfect love drives out fear. . . . The man who fears is not made perfect in love.

Your Father
(Prov. 11:24-26; 1 Cor. 13:1-8; 2 Tim. 1:7; 1 John 4:18)

48
With Love, Marsha

Dear Father:

I arrived at the office early one day and saw something special. In the middle of the stacks of memos and paper that embedded my office was a solitary rose—right on top of a "to-do" list. The card said, "I love you." The rose drew my focus away from the many memos and stacks of unanswered correspondence—I was loved!

The days passed. The collection of days resulted in weeks, and weeks turned into months. Each day, a new rose appeared. The message was the same: "I love you." It never appeared in the same place twice. One day it was attached to the windshield wiper of my car. On another, it was in the mailbox. It was always unexpected, yet always welcome. The inconsistency of where it turned up was made special by the consistency of what it said: I was loved.

Something marvelous happens when we are loved. My self-esteem soared. I was worthy of attention. I felt like someone special—a queen. And he was my king!

Then it happened. Change. While change is the most expected part of life, I was not prepared to lose my love. I wanted to hold tightly to that which gave me a sense of well-being, purpose, and value. But just as I struggled to hold on to my love, the relationship dissolved. *If I had seen it coming, could I have done something different?* I wondered.

That's when You came, Father. Your letters helped soothe the pain of loss. I remember reading Your love letters as I searched for love to fill the void. There, in the pages of Your letters, I found comfort. I found love again. But, maybe not *again.* Perhaps I experienced love for the first time when I came to know Your love.

I did not need Your view of love, for my view of love was working well—until it changed, that is. I was reminded of the poet Alfred, Lord Tennyson, "'Tis better to have loved and lost than never to have loved at all." I was not sure.

I had always thought of love as a trade agreement. If I was good enough, pretty enough, and smart enough, I was loved. This was rooted in my immature understanding that love depended on who I was, who I was with, what I looked like, and what I did. If any of those changed, I would lose my love.

With a desperate heart to know love, I escaped to my private sanctuary—the beach. There, I began to scan Your love letters. That is when I

49
A Time to Love

learned the essence of love. To know You is to know love. And Your love is radically different from the world's view of it.

You love me not because of who I am, but because of who You are. You are love.

You love me not because of what I do. If that were the case and I no longer did that, then You could not love me. You are love.

You love me not because of where I am. If that were the case and I were no longer there, You could not love me. You are love.

You love me not because of who I am with. If that were the case and I were no longer with that person, You could not love me. You are love.

You love me not because of how I look. If that were the case and I no longer looked the same, You could not love me. You are love.

You love me simply because you have said, I am love.

I remember exactly the moment You taught me that incredible lesson about Your consistent love. I sat alone for hours on the white sand. It was safer that way. I needed to read Your letters again and again to sort through my feelings. After reading them one by one, just as the sunshine warms and heals the skin, you began to penetrate my heart. It began to feel warm again as healing began. Quietly, I placed Your letters on the beach. I spent the entire day, sitting with You in love. Then the moment came when I felt Your touch. Gently, You reached Your hands toward me and spoke in a voice that only my desperate heart could hear, "Let Me love you." With courage, I accepted Your gift of love. I entwined my heart around it. It was wrought by the wisdom of the Holy Spirit.

Before I gathered Your letters and my blanket, I was reminded that the only way to sense Your love is to give it away. I could not give away what I did not have. By giving love, I would prove that I was loved.

Father, continue to remind me of the plain essence of love. To have a constant sense of your love, I must give my love away.

With love,
Marsha

That None Shall Be Lost

Dear Child:
What do you think? If a man owns a hundred sheep, and one of them wanders away, will he not leave the ninety-nine on the hills and go to look for the one that wandered off? And if he finds it, I tell you the truth, he is happier about that one sheep than about the ninety-nine that did not wander off. In the same way your Father in heaven is not willing that any of these little ones should be lost.

I tell you, open your eyes and look at the fields! They are ripe for harvest.

Your Father
(Matt. 18:12-14; John 4:35)

51
That None Shall Be Lost

Dear Father:

It has happened before, but not as intensely as today. As I entered the coffee shop, a familiar-looking woman greeted me. We exchanged looks. I am certain we both thought, *Don't I know you from somewhere?* The tall woman seated me at a booth near the window. *How did she know I liked window seats?* I thought.

"Coffee only," I ordered as I pulled out my notes for today's seminar.

"Somehow I knew that," was her immediate response.

I had been drinking coffee and working for several minutes when she came to refill my cup. She was so attentive and commented, "I know you're busy, but can I ask you a question?"

I looked up.

"Well, I feel like I know you from somewhere. I was back in the kitchen telling Sara Ann, the other waitress, about you. She said, 'Ethel, just go up and ask her.' So, I'm asking. Where could we have met?" the waitress inquired.

"It's strange that you should say that," I came back. "I had those same feelings. In fact, I thought about it and decided maybe you just reminded me of someone else. After all, I don't even live here. I live in Birmingham, Alabama."

"I've never even been to Alabama," Ethel replied.

Quickly I responded, "But I used to live here in Fort Worth. It's been ten years," I told her.

"No, that's not it," Ethel said. "I didn't live here then. In fact, I just moved from Dallas to Fort Worth a few months ago," she replied.

"Dallas! You lived in Dallas? That's it," I concluded.

Ethel responded quickly, "I was transferred from the coffee shop on Forest Lane to this one about a year ago."

"Ethel, don't you remember me? The one with the books. You served me coffee after seating me by the window while I studied," I almost shouted.

"Of course! I wondered whatever happened to you," Ethel said suddenly. "You disappeared. You look so different in *real clothes,*" she laughed.

"Can you sit down for a minute? We must catch up," I told her.

Ethel sat there for over an hour as we talked. I shared about my life, she about hers. It was a fascinating experience. I recall our closing words before I had to leave her:

"Ethel, you're delightful. How could I have missed knowing you all that time?" I asked.

Ethel stared out the window as the sun began to shimmer through the blue-and-purple Texas sky. "Well, I really wanted to talk to you so many times in Dallas. In fact, we all talked about you back in the kitchen. No one could understand why anyone would get up so early and spend so much time studying. We were fascinated, to say the least. But you never looked up. In fact, I don't think you ever saw me."

Father, I could not respond. I knew Ethel was right. I had not seen her. My world was focused on my self-centered inner being and personal goals. I remember my ambition. How else could I have done it? The alarm jolted me from my warm bed at precisely 4:15 a.m. The routine was like clockwork. By 4:30 a.m., I was dressed in my warm-ups and walking out the door of my condo toward my car. By 4:45, I entered the coffee shop only one block from home. My arms were always loaded with a stack of books and a blue notebook. Fortunately for me, the restaurant was open twenty-four hours.

Each morning, Ethel seated me at the same booth by the window. She was tall, slender, and in her mid-forties. That's about all I remembered. After all, it took all of my mental energy to be awake, much less notice anyone else. We exchanged little conversation except, "I'll have your coffee out in one second." And, she did just that—she kept my cup filled.

From 4:40 until 6:30, I sat in that booth, glued to the stack of books while I consumed numerous cups of coffee. I seldom focused my eyes away from my reason for being there.

Earlier that year, I had decided to return to school. I already had a graduate degree but realized that to have a more effective ministry with adults, I needed more education. This meant sacrifice. I could not afford the luxury of resigning my job to attend school full-time. This meant squeezing in study time. I had to prepare for the famous Graduate Record Exam.

So, each morning I studied. Within four months, I had memorized 4,000 vocabulary words, relearned geometry and algebra, practiced thinking analytically, and polished reading comprehension skills. I

53
That None Shall Be Lost

spent every moment studying when I wasn't at work. I carried vocabulary words on index cards and reviewed them while waiting in grocery lines. The challenge almost became an obsession.

While my focus grew on my noble ambition, I focused less on my outer world. I had set priorities. These priorities did not include people, for the time being anyway.

Father, somehow I want to preserve today's bright encounter with Ethel. I realized that, as a rule, truly enlightening experiences happen out of the ordinary and can even occur when one is half-asleep. It is often in the commonplace of our everydayness—the routines of life—that encounters become memorable—so memorable that perhaps they can change us for the rest of our lives.

Yet, how often do I become so caught up in my "spiritual" or noble affairs that I miss seeing the obvious—the spiritual needs right around me. Sometimes I miss them because of my prejudices or the inconvenience they cause.

Father, I need help in keeping my focus on others. How many Ethels are living in my world today to whom I could minister? Forgive me for not seeing because my focus has been off center. My attention has been on myself. Yet, thinking about my outer world terrifies me. How can I possibly meet all the needs out there?

The focus in Your letters is clear. I live in only one physical world, one place, and one moment at a time. If I could focus on my own world and if other Christians did the same, together we could reach the world for You.

Father, teach me to focus on the world outside myself. Only then am I fulfilling that which I have been redeemed to do. Only when I am aware of the Ethels can I be fully aware of who You are.

With love,
Marsha

The Teacher

Dear Child:
    A student is not above his teacher, nor a servant above his master. It is enough for the student to be like his teacher, and the servant like his master.
    For you have one Teacher, the Christ.
    For the Holy Spirit will teach you at that time what you should say.
    But the Counselor, the Holy Spirit, whom the Father will send in my name, will teach you all things and will remind you of everything I have said to you.
    You, then, who teach others, do you not teach yourself?
    I will instruct you and teach you in the way you should go; I will counsel you and watch over you.
    Teach me, O Lord, to follow your decrees; then I will keep them to the end.

Your Father
(Matt. 10:24-25; 23:10; Luke 12:12; John 14:26; Rom. 2:21; Pss. 32:8; 119:33)

55
The Teacher

Dear Father:

I could hardly wait for the retreat to start. I was the first one to slide across the icy driveway to the large conference room where I would teach the two-day seminar. I wanted to gain a head start by setting up my materials and developing a feel for the room. I also had tucked inside the hope of fresh coffee and a warm fireplace. As soon as I entered, I was greeted by coffee, a warm fire, and two women who had beat me to the conference room. They, too, could hardly wait!

At first I thought they were the cleaning crew or maybe the cooks. They certainly did not look like the people I expected to attend my conference. They were warm, outgoing, confident, and genuine in their interest toward me. Yet, these two did not look like people I would want to run into in a dark alley at night. Their dress was unusual—chains and huge black belts, tank tops, and matching boots. Their hair was messy, and their faces were extremely plain and rugged. Their arms shocked me the most. Tattoos!

Who are these women? What are they doing here? This is a Christian women's meeting. They are nice, but they certainly don't look like any women who have been to my seminars before, I thought.

I poured a cup of coffee as I realized they were there by choice. As I opened my bag to pull out conference materials, they eagerly volunteered to help put them in the chairs. That is when I introduced myself.

"Good morning, I'm Marsha Spradlin," I announced.

"We know who you are," one of the women answered. "We saw your picture in the brochure. We can't wait to start. That's why we're here early."

Thoughts of a room full of such women frightened me. I felt intimidated. I wasn't sure how to communicate with these "different" women. I felt unsure about how well they would receive me as their teacher. I seemingly had nothing in common with them.

Moments later, the retreat coordinator walked in to greet me. I felt relieved. She invited me to a tiny office to review the schedule.

"I guess you're wondering about those two," she noted.

"Wondering? Yes! Who are they?" I asked.

"They are among the most active and committed young Christian women in our state right now. I know that is hard to believe, but they have a testimony that has touched the lives of others like them—the street people," Jane, the conference coordinator, continued to explain. "Sandra and Helen are sisters. I expect there will be others like them here. If I know Helen and Sandra, they have invited their friends. Anyway, Sandra and Helen grew up in a Christian home. Like so many kids these days, they became sidetracked in high school. They became involved with the wrong crowd, I guess. Before long, they were skipping church, school, and family functions like meals. That's when their parents began to get a little suspicious. Sandra and Helen had made friends with the drug culture. Well, it's a horrible story.

"Several months ago, in fact, a year next month, their mother was diagnosed with a terminal illness. Sandra and Helen were, of course, upset about their mother whom they had neglected. They decided to do what they had always been taught. They prayed. They asked God to heal their mom. In fact, they made a deal: 'God, if you make our mom well, we will get back into church.' Now, Marsha, I do not agree with this theology. I mean, you can't buy favors with God. He's not a contract worker, but I can't knock what they did. It worked for them.

"Regardless, their mother did get well. A full recovery. The two girls kept their end of the bargain. In fact, they rededicated their lives, gave up drugs, and began a ministry to the drug community. It is not uncommon to have two church pews filled with tattooed gals and guys in black jackets and belts Sunday morning in their church," Jane reported.

As the retreat got underway, I could not help noticing the commitment of these two. They were determined to make a winning difference in their world. Was the commitment a response to fear, oughts, or shoulds, or was it results, desire, and love? The answer became obvious to me. Their commitment was grounded in assuming responsibility for their lost world. Their commitment resulted in action. They may have looked like street people on the outside, but on the inside, they were making positive steps to renew their hearts and minds. Their actions spoke louder than words. They taught this teacher about ministry and witness.

Father, Sandra and Helen taught me an extraordinary lesson. We may not be able to touch every life, but we can touch the lives of those persons nearest us—our world. In order to touch such lives, we cannot

The Teacher

separate ourselves from the world physically, but we must separate ourselves spiritually. That is the winning difference. That is what made Helen and Sandra different from their non-Christian friends. My purpose at the retreat was to be the teacher. Instead, I became the learner.

Father, You are the authority on teaching. You sent Your Son to be the Master Teacher. As I scan Your letters, I find many examples of His teaching methods. For example, in teaching the woman at the well, Jesus used questions and answers. With the leper, Jesus performed a miracle, an example of demonstrative teaching. With the multitudes, Jesus delivered a speech, an example of the lecture method. With others He listened, touched, and cared. His teacher/pupil ratio ranged from one to one to one and the multitude. But, like Sandra and Helen, wherever He was, He taught with kindness. He always anticipated the needs of His learners. He always met them where they were.

Your letters clearly underscore that it is Your will that all people are to be taught about You and come to know Your truth. Again, Jesus' life is the perfect example. He took risks. He was not afraid to touch and be touched. He touched and healed the man suffering from leprosy. Can I be so brave?

Jesus was sensitive. Your letters give many accounts of His sensitivity. He was tired and needed rest, but He was sensitive to those who demonstrated a readiness to learn. While teaching spiritual truths, Jesus recognized the physical needs of His learners. He fed the multitudes with five loaves and two fishes. Then He taught. Do I often use the excuse that I am too tired to teach in Your name?

Jesus taught wherever He was. Your letter about the blind man, Bartimaeus, is an example. As Jesus left the city, the blind man pleaded for Him to stop and have mercy on him. Jesus did pause, and the blind man was healed. Do I ever get too busy to minister right where I am?

Father, teach me to be a teacher. Teach me to take risks and to be sensitive. Make my life a teaching model that ministers and teaches wherever I am. May I learn from Jesus' example to take courage in reaching out, demonstrating untiring sensitivity, and ministering wherever I go, only then do I demonstrate what it means to be Your child.

With love,
Marsha

A Divine Intervention

Dear Child:

You will receive power when the Holy Spirit comes on you; and you will be my witnesses in Jerusalem, and in all Judea and Samaria, and to the ends of the earth.

But if he will not listen, take one or two others along, so that every matter may be established by the testimony of two or three witnesses.

We accept man's testimony, but God's testimony is greater because it is the testimony of God, which he has given about his Son. Anyone who believes in the Son of God has this testimony in his heart.

A truthful witness gives honest testimony.

Your Father
(Acts 1:8; Matt. 18:16; 1 John 5:9-10; Prov. 12:17)

59
A Divine Intervention

Dear Father:

Jan was not intentionally eavesdropping this morning, but it was obvious she had overheard every word of my conversation with Vicky, a waitress in the coffee shop. Perhaps Jan had sensed openness and acceptance from the conversation. Maybe she was so lonely that mere visual contact with someone made her feel warmhearted.

I noticed Jan and felt she wanted an invitation to join us at our table. As Vicky left to continue her responsibilities, I signaled for Jan to join me. Speaking quietly, she said, "I heard what you told that waitress. Will it work for me, too?"

I marveled at the presence of Your Spirit. I knew it was You who synchronized our lives to meet in this time and place. My new acquaintance with Jan reinforced my conviction that people are starved for answers regarding life. Only You, Father, have answers to life's perplexities.

What Jan overheard was only one of a series of fifteen-minute visits with Vicky. For over a year, I have stopped for coffee before going to work. Through these frequent "touchpoints," Vicky and I have become more than acquaintances. We are friends. Although our visits have covered a variety of topics, our conversation this morning focused on You. I had just shared with Vicky Your plan of salvation. It is now evident that this morning's witness to Vicky was a vicarious presentation to Jan.

As Jan introduced herself, I noticed a real quiver in her voice. She seemed shy and afraid. Even though she was not especially attractive physically, she had an inner beauty. I recognized potential. It was not long until I knew some of Jan's background, life-style, and struggles. Her emotions were tender. She appeared to be literally dying for love and attention. "On this very morning," she confessed, "I tried to kill myself." Jan shared why she had lost hope, because of some deep-seated problems that had collected over the years.

I am convinced You, Father, are bigger than any problem we have. As I shared this with Jan, I realized she caught a spark of hope. After an hour, I recognized that Jan faced many decisions. The most important one concerned her personal relationship with You. I walked Jan to her car and slipped a New Testament into her hand. I focused my eyes intensely into hers and said, "I love you."

60
With Love, Marsha

She sat in her parked car with her head buried in her hands for what seemed an eternity. I observed her from my car and prayed that she was putting her trust in You. As she drove away, I immediately realized that I might never see her again. I also was aware that through Jesus Christ, we could spend eternity together for we had just then encountered Your presence.

I am more convinced than ever that the reason for my very existence is to meet ordinary people on ordinary days. I am equally convinced that the reason You ushered Jan into my life today was simply to let me fulfill Your Great Commission and be a witness right where I am.

As I reread Your letters to discover how Jesus made a winning difference in His world, I have not found a formula. What I discovered is that He shared through ordinary, plain-vanilla, everyday experiences.

Father, if I choose to make a difference in my world, I must learn to touch as Jesus did. He touched people daily—not merely in signs and wonders and miracles—but also in the ordinary moments of life. His touch came from deep within. If I choose to make a difference in the world, I must join other Christians. Together we can make a bold, winning team that is not afraid to touch.

Father, what does a winning touch look like, feel like, act like? Being a witness starts in attitude, doesn't it? Unlike physical life in which we are not born equally—heredity has no uniform—spiritually we are all capable of becoming genuine witnesses—I like the old-fashioned term, "soul-winners."

I know, Father, that environment does not always breed and nurture the witnessing spirit; yet, as I celebrate You within, I celebrate the Savior, Your only begotten Son, the God-man who every day makes a difference in my life. Through such celebration, I become a living example as to Christ's power to change lives, not only the Jans but also the Marshas. Springing out of Your greatness is an overflow of Your love that can transform the entire world. May my life be a witness every day.

With love,
Marsha

Unto Me

Dear Child:

I was hungry and you gave me something to eat, I was thirsty and you gave me something to drink, . . . I needed clothes and you clothed me, I was sick and you looked after me, I was in prison and you came to visit me.

Then the righteous will answer him, "Lord, when did we see you hungry and feed you, or thirsty and give you something to drink? When did we see you a stranger and invite you in, or needed clothes and clothe you? When did we see you sick or in prison and go to visit you?"

I tell you the truth, whatever you did for one of the least of these brothers of mine, you did for me.

Your Father
(Matt. 25:35-40)

With Love, Marsha

Dear Father:

Today is Easter morning. Driving home from church today triggered the memory of the most meaningful Easter of my life. On that Sunday, You taught me the real meaning of Easter and life's purpose. I was no older than ten, but the impressions are permanently inscribed in my heart and mind.

My family was driving home from church when we saw a man sitting under a tree near the highway. He was old, obviously malnourished, and not adequately dressed for the unexpected cold weather on this spring morning. I still remember my feelings as I observed Mother and Daddy's spontaneous, yet nonverbal, expressions of concern. The mute-like silence was not broken until we arrived home several minutes later.

Sunday lunch was always special. I remember in detail the meal my mother prepared that day: roast beef, mashed potatoes, green beans, and chocolate cake with little pecans sprinkled on top. We were trying to enjoy our Sunday meal when Daddy suddenly excused himself. We knew where he was going. We knew our father.

Now, nearly twenty-five years later, my emotions are touched as I remember how I felt when he returned to the table fifteen minutes later. The old man was with him. The old man smelled as if he had not bathed in weeks. I suddenly lost my appetite, but I recall that another appetite was stimulated as I watched my parents demonstrate Your love. I remember how I felt when Mother gave our guest an enormous plate of food, plus a large piece of cake and glass of milk. I also remember how I felt when Daddy pulled out his wallet and gave the old man a ten-dollar bill before driving him to the community relief shelter.

For hours after the man left our home, our family discussed the experience. I still remember my younger brother's question, "Why did we do that?"

I likewise remember Daddy's response, "Son, how could we not do it?"

The experience made an incredible impression on three children. What we felt that day was inscribed on our memories. I am grateful that my parents demonstrated missions rather than going through the motions of primly explaining to us the meaning of the word.

Father, I have a responsibility to demonstrate missions every day. Whatever we have learned from godly parents or other Christians, will

63
Unto Me

require action. If I do not demonstrate Your love, I question if I have ever experienced it. Make my life not only a vessel to contain love but a vehicle that demonstrates and distributes it to "one of the least of these."

With love,
Marsha

A Severe Joy

Dear Child:
   You will fill me with joy in your presence, with eternal pleasures at your right hand.
   How great is his joy in the victories you give!
   My lips will shout for joy when I sing praise to you—I, whom you have redeemed.
   For you make me glad by your deeds, O Lord; I sing for joy at the works of your hands.
   The Lord has done great things for us, and we are filled with joy.
   I have told you this so that my joy may be in you and that your joy may be complete.
   I tell you the truth, you will weep and mourn while the world rejoices. You will grieve, but your grief will turn to joy. . . . So with you: Now is your time of grief, but I will see you again and you will rejoice, and no one will take away your joy.
   May the God of hope fill you with all joy and peace as you trust in him, so that you may overflow with hope by the power of the Holy Spirit.

Your Father
(Pss. 16:11; 21:1; 71:23; 92:4; 126:3; John 15:11; 16:20,22; Rom. 15:13)

A Severe Joy

Dear Father:

How well I recall how my perception of joy was deeply tested. I received the devastating news that Daddy had undergone a severe stroke. Within hours I was on a plane to Mobile, Alabama, to join my family in a crisis unlike any we had previously experienced. When I arrived, I was greeted by at least fifty friends—friends of Dad's who had come to the hospital to support, encourage, and join in our pain. He was in surgery for nearly five hours. We had been told that he had a 50 percent chance to live through surgery. He made it! Then we learned that he might never regain consciousness and, if he did, he might never know us. The news was hard to hear and comprehend.

At 2:00 a.m. the following morning, my mother, sister, sister-in-law, and I walked to the car. We decided to put Daddy into Your hands. My brother stayed at the hospital while we went home for a few hours of much-needed sleep. I shall never forget Mother's comment as we walked arm in arm to the car: "I can't believe I am leaving my husband in this hospital. I am going home to sleep. Why do I feel so relaxed and at peace? I should be in misery."

Cindy, my sister-in-law, quickly responded: "Wanda, the miracle of real joy comes in the midst of the storm. Remember the people who greeted us and held our hands during those hours of surgery? God is answering their prayers to grant us peace and joy in the midst of our misery."

Dad did regain consciousness after a six-week coma. He is a walking testimony of the joy that comes through faith in the midst of the storm. But, for me, Heavenly Father, there were many unjoyful moments during those weeks. I questioned You as I watched Daddy suffer and thought about the uncertainties ahead. What is joy? Is it the same as happiness?

To help me regain perspective on the meaning of joy, I read Your letters many times. I began to think about the person I enjoyed being with the most. As I thought, I could call to mind more than one person. While each one was different, there was one quality that stood out. Each was joyful.

Joy is contagious. I am attracted to joyful people. When I have undergone a no-good, very bad day, the last person I prefer to be with is

With Love, Marsha

what I call a NIOP. NIOPs are those who have a negative influence on people. Their every action is the antithesis of joy.

Your letters speak plentifully about joy, but strangely enough, nowhere do they speak about a "happy" Christian. I know that happiness and joy are not synonyms.

I once heard that joy is not something to seek after; it is something experienced only in the moment. I believe that is true. Joy is not a destination, nor is it an emotion to be sought; instead, joy is in the journey. I experience joy as I become rightly related to You.

This truth opposes the world's view of joy. I began to observe the number of messages, commercials, and advertisement campaigns that insist that joy can be bought. The secular view of a joyful life insists that joy comes through possessions. Therefore, the world's goal and determination are to make me as unjoyful as possible. I am bombarded daily with messages that insist that I am living a life of lack and limitation. The message is clear: If I only had a particular brand of product or possession, joy would instantly be produced in my life.

I must admit, I continue to fight daily this secular concept of joy. I become caught up in the "someday I'll have" or "someday I'll be" mind-set. When I concentrate on the someday, I lose sight of the now.

I remember the years when I lived in North Dallas, Texas. Today, I would call this area the "yuppie" community. Yuppies are "supposed" to have high-tech equipment, like this computer I'm using for this letter and valuable antiques accentuating their homes. Yuppies drive BMWs, wear 100 percent cotton, starched shirts, and live in patio homes with neatly manicured lots. While I did not have a BMW or a patio home, I must admit I did drop by the BMW dealership near my third-floor condominium on occasion. My definition of joy began to become blown out of proportion. In retrospect, I realize there is truly nothing wrong with having things, but when things become a vehicle to obtain joy, well, we are on the road to losing. We lose our joy.

Joy is deeper than what I have or what I wear. It is a life-style consistent with that of Jesus Christ. The joy of Jesus was the total self-surrender and self-sacrifice of Himself to the will of His Father, the joy of doing exactly what the Father sent Him to do. I can see two threads tightly woven—the thread of joy and the thread of will.

Joy comes into my life when it is merged with Your life, Father. My

67
A Severe Joy

goal should not be joy, peace, or blessing, but You alone! Joy is the stronghold of our Christian faith. It is the miracle of the Christian life. Such miracles can be seen when we experience joy in the midst of external misery.

How do I obtain the kind of joy that is contagious? Since the days of Daddy's illness, You have taught me that joy comes only when I allow You to fulfill Your design in and through me. Joy, therefore, lies in fulfilling Your purpose for creating me. I fulfill this design when I am at one with You, Father. Then the Spirit of God fills me and gives me that overflowing sense of joy. Joy is the result of being what I am created to be—like Your Son. Joy has nothing to do with what is happening around me. Joy is literally Your nature in me. It is here that I can tap into the true energy for living a victorious life. It is here that others notice a valuable difference in my life.

Again, joy isn't to be sought ambitiously, but peacefully, as I grow in the likeness of the Lord Jesus. May my life reflect sincere joy as I become more like You, Lord.

With love,
Marsha

Two Doors Down

Dear Child:

Restore us, O God; make your face shine upon us, that we may be saved.

He leads me beside quiet waters, he restores my soul. He guides me in paths of righteousness for his name's sake.

Restore us to yourself, O Lord, that we may return: renew our days as of old unless you have utterly rejected us and are angry with us beyond measure.

Your Father
(Pss. 80:3; 23:2; Lam. 5:21)

Two Doors Down

Dear Father:

Your letter today reminded me of the restoration occurring in my own world. Two doors down my street is a wonderful old house—tall columns, two stories, sixteen windows, distinct architectural features. For nearly two months, I have watched the restoration team strip the paint off the sides of that nearly seventy-year-old house. The once-strong columns are now supported by two-by-fours. Scaffolding towers over the shrubs which have been draped with sheets to protect them from debris. The house is in a period of transition.

Even though I was not aware the house needed repairs, the owners were. They were willing to pay to have this old building repaired. The price involved more than financial expenses. It meant parking on the street rather than in the garage, stepping over paint cans, and living in the house that was the talk of the neighborhood—the one with no seeming aesthetic value.

But the restoration period will be over soon. The once-beautiful old home will regain its beauty. It will not only be attached to the surface, it will penetrate the house's very core and foundation. The result will be added strength, value, and an increased lifespan.

Three doors down my street lived a lovely woman. She was attractive, strong, and appeared to be in excellent health. For nearly a year, I watched her come and go. I wondered if she, like the house, needed internal restoration or support. I sensed an internal struggle.

After a year of exchanging "good morning," I invited her in for coffee. She accepted. As I opened the door, I likewise opened my heart to Janie. We visited for hours on that Saturday morning. Inside that beautiful woman was one tormented by failure, limitations, and lack of relationship with You, Father. Perhaps because of her pain, she was willing to pay the price to find relief, help, and total restoration.

As we discussed Your ability to rebuild, I was reminded of Psalm 139. You made us; certainly You can put the complicated and delicate pieces back together. But there is still the cost. Unlike the house, the cost of Janie's internal restoration had already been paid through Jesus Christ. Janie accepted the challenge to seek restoration through You.

During the following months, Janie became the talk of the neighborhood. The change could not be contained. It was evident by her joy and

With Love, Marsha

life-style. The restoration went all the way to her internal core and foundation. Because Jesus Christ now controlled her life, she was confident that her value had increased. This confidence gave her strength. She was equally confident that she would now live forever.

Father, teach me about doors—those unique opportunities to enter someone's life in Your name. Help me to seek "doors" and be willing not only to go inside but also to stay as I have opportunities to develop relationships. Help me to be willing to allow the door to open in both directions. Help me to be willing to share myself as I continue to follow Your footsteps.

With love,
Marsha

The Gardener

Dear Child:

I planted the seed, Apollos watered it, but God made it grow. So neither he who plants nor he who waters is anything, but only God, who makes things grow. The man who plants and the man who waters have one purpose, and each will be rewarded according to his own labor. For we are God's fellow workers, you are God's field, God's building.

A farmer went out to sow his seed. Still other seed fell on good soil, where it produced a crop—a hundred, sixty or thirty times what was sown. He who has ears, let him hear.

The seed is the word of God. Those along the path are the ones who hear.

Your Father
(1 Cor. 3:6-9; Matt. 13:3*b*,8-9; Luke 8:11-12)

With Love, Marsha

Dear Father:

It's spring—a time for planting seeds. Thank You for the opportunity to plant a seed today. The seed was planted on the return flight from a weekend retreat for women this weekend. My seat belt was buckled and headphones plugged in as I anticipated a productive flight. I had given much of myself, but I had received much more. As I saw young women at the retreat recognize and respond to Your leadership, I, too, was called to a deeper level of commitment and responsibility. Perhaps it was the overflow of Your nourishment during the retreat that caused me to notice Sharon and David.

The 727 was ready to take off when they made their way down the crowded aisle to the only two empty seats. I quickly gathered my belongings from the seats next to me. Sharon, an attractive woman in her mid-thirties, and David, her active twelve-year-old son, were returning from a weekend vacation. We were strangers but seemed to have a common interest in becoming acquainted.

As the plane taxied, I observed Sharon's need to talk. I put away my headphones and manuscripts and prayed to You, Father, that if this family needed some of the overflow (and I could just plant a seed) that You'd let me be a tool in sharing and planting Your love.

Thank you, kind Father, for responding so quickly to my prayer. The hours passed quickly. My ears and eyes were instruments that recognized Sharon's request for love. My heart was filled with compassion as I realized Your power within. My mouth became a channel that shared the message of hope to these newfound friends. I relied totally on Your Spirit within me today.

Sharon was a victim of dreadful experiences. She and David had gone on a spring vacation, temporarily to escape some of their pain. Not only had Sharon recently experienced a divorce, but she also had just lost a seventeen-year-old son in a hunting accident. As she poured out her grief, my overflow seemed to surround her. She now seemed to feel safe, loved, and accepted. Because of such acceptance, Sharon was interested in any words of encouragement. Sharing what You had done in my life was easy and natural. We cried and prayed together before saying goodbye in Atlanta.

Father, I realize that not every contact with a lost person brings such a spontaneous opportunity to witness, but I am deeply convinced that a

The Gardener

witness from the overflow is by far the most effective kind. Like your letters explained to me, my job is to plant the seed, but I recognize that I cannot plant what I do not have. Thank you for the overflow.

Where does such an overflow come from? You have taught me that my overflow, or gardening ability, comes by spending time in Your garden. As I come to Your garden, I merge my mind, heart, and time with You. My actions often become a spontaneous, direct response to that which dominates my thoughts. I usually do or become that which I think about most often. Maybe that is why You stress, "Whatever is true, whatever is noble, whatever is right, whatever is pure, whatever is lovely, whatever is admirable—if anything is excellent or praiseworthy—think about such things" (Phil. 4:8).

You have taught me that preparation for planting seeds comes as I merge my mind, heart, and time. These must be intentional actions with internal and eternal implications. As I spend time in Your garden through reading Your letters and listening to what is written between each line, I train my mind to see with Your eyes. I develop a life-style of overflow out of which I recognize needs and respond quickly by planting a seed. I rely on You, Father, then to nurture, water, and reap.

Make me Your gardener. Start by cultivating the inner garden within my own heart and soul. Help me identify weeds. Turn the soil, pull out the unwanted growth, use the soil You have given me in which to plant seeds that You will water and nourish. Make my garden a delicate place, properly maintained, and not overrun by intrusive undergrowth.

Make my garden a place where we can visit and a place where I can grow. May the center of my garden become a place where Your spirit comes to make self-disclosure, share wisdom, give affirmation or rebuke, provide encouragement, and give direction and guidance.

I know You do not often walk in disordered gardens. May my garden be one in which You always feel welcome. May You enjoy the harvest that results.

With love,
Marsha

Perfect Timing

Dear Child:
   There is a time for everything, and a season for every activity under heaven: a time to be born and a time to die, a time to plant and a time to uproot, a time to kill and a time to heal, a time to tear down and a time to build, a time to weep and a time to laugh, a time to mourn and a time to dance, a time to scatter stones and a time to gather them, a time to embrace and a time to refrain, a time to search and a time to give up, a time to keep and a time to throw away, a time to tear and a time to mend, a time to be silent and a time to speak, a time to love and a time to hate, a time for war and a time for peace. He has made everything beautiful in its time.
   The wise heart will know the proper time and procedure. For there is a proper time and procedure for every matter.
   It is time to seek the Lord, until he comes and showers righteousness on you.
   And do this, understanding the present time. The hour has come for you to wake up from your slumber, because our salvation is nearer now than when we first believed.
   But I trust in you, O Lord; I say, "You are my God." My times are in your hands; deliver me from my enemies and from those who pursue me.

Your Father
(Eccl. 3:1-8,11; 8:5-6; Hos. 10:12-13; Rom. 13:11; Ps. 31:14-15)

75
Perfect Timing

Dear Father:

I have barely enough time to write You before making the early flight home. If I don't make it, it really is OK. I seem to have an unwritten agreement with the airline. If I am not at the airport on time, they go ahead without me.

Your letter this morning about time captured my attention all day. Time may be a potent healer, but it's not the world's most marvelous beautifier!

Yes, Father, time is interesting to me. Sometimes, I have noticed that some people can stay longer in one day than other people can stay in a whole week! It is all in one's perspective of time.

Now that I have time to think, my mind wants to race ahead toward tomorrow's schedule. It is as if I want a head start on it! Tomorrow is jam-packed. In fact, the list of deeds I have to accomplish is running over. No, wait a minute. The list is not running over; I am!

I must simplify my life. Time is running out, and I am trying to pack as much into life as quickly as possible. Courses in time management have taught me ways to compensate time, manage time, and save time. But I am not sure any one of these fits into Your schedule of managing the time of my life. Time-savers include a microwave oven, the express lane in the grocery store, as well as the automatic bank teller. All are supposed to save time. Yet, I manage to pack more miscellany into the time I have saved. Have I really saved any?

I have learned to make time by arising one hour earlier each day. That adds up to one extra day each month! If time is money, I should be producing a little extra income.

The tyranny of the urgent is gnawing at my day—bit by bit. There seems to be no life left. My life has become more of a life of trivial pursuit. I don't feel I have breathing room, *much less being room.*

Father, teach me that now is the only time there is. I am embarrassed to admit I have become so wrapped up in saving time that I am not sure I know what day it is. Teach me that today is not confined to a calendar or a "to-do" list. Today is today.

I took a moment and put my pen down to look outside the airport window. I saw today. It is decidedly different from any other day I have ever lived. You have given me only today to experience the exact people

With Love, Marsha

I need to meet and the places I need to go. I can never go back and retrieve today. It is here only now.

Within today, You have sheathed all of the good and perfect gifts You wish to give me. Yet, I am responsible for recognizing it. To live today is my choice. I can either use it, or I can become so wrapped in it that I lose it.

Is it true, Father, that in order to have time, I must just live time? And to have life, I must give myself and my time away? If so, the only way to increase my time is to give it away! To increase my life, I must invest it in others. It sounds too simple.

This has been called the "Star Trek" generation. I combat constantly the need to be in two places at once. With modern technological advances, "warp time" seems almost a reality.

Warp time is the remarkable, yet imaginary, ability to go forward in time instantly as well as backward. The implications are incredible. I could go back in time to recapture witnessing opportunities I missed due to lack of awareness of Your meaning of *now*. I could also go forward in time or to the "ends of the earth" instantly with Your message. As incredible as warp time may be, however, it is not possible. I cannot go backward or forward in time, nor can I be in two places at once.

I am here—now! It is only the here and now for which I am responsible. Teach me, Father, to act responsibly with those persons within my world. Teach me to act now. By living responsibly, I can become all You have designed for me to be. I am more like me when I am doing Your will than at any other time.

I could spend these next moments regretting that I have not acted responsibly in the use of my time for You. Instead, Father, free me to start right now being responsible for the time that is now and for the people within my world right now. Yes, Father, You have made all things beautiful in Your own time. Only as I give to you the many moments of my today can You make me move in synch with Your "perfect timing."

With love,
Marsha

A Magnificent Encounter

Dear Child:

Let the Lord judge the peoples. Judge me, O Lord, according to my righteousness, according to my integrity, O Most High.

Do not judge, or you too will be judged. For in the same way you judge others, you will be judged, and with the measure you use, it will be measured to you.

For I did not come to judge the world, but to save it.

You, then, why do you judge your brother? Or why do you look down on your brother? For we will all stand before God's judgment seat.

Therefore judge nothing before the appointed time; wait till the Lord comes. He will bring to light what is hidden in darkness and will expose the motives of men's hearts. At that time each will receive his praise from God.

As for those who seemed to be important—whatever they were makes no difference to me; God does not judge by external appearance.

There is only one Lawgiver and Judge, the one who is able to save and destroy. But you—who are you to judge your neighbor?

Your Father
(Ps. 7:8; Matt. 7:1-2; John 12:47; Rom. 14:10; 1 Cor. 4:5; Gal. 2:6; Jas. 4:12)

78
With Love, Marsha

Dear Father:

This is a late-night letter written from the heavens. I estimate I am now about 32,000 feet above sea level. The flight left at midnight Alabama time. I've already been in the air more than twelve hours. Only a few more minutes remain on the final leg of this trip from Anchorage, Alaska, to Birmingham. I must admit I began this day of travel tired, spent, and eager to make it home. But I feel a "good tired." The week in Alaska leading seminars, speaking, and consulting has been well spent. As usual, I feel like I'm the one who received the greatest blessing!

I needed to rest, but sleep was difficult on the plane. This particular flight schedule was called the "milk run." I believe we stopped and/or changed planes in nearly every airport from Portland eastward. Midway through the trip, in Dallas, I believe, I boarded one of the last planes of the journey. That is where I met Gabby.

She was bundled in a blanket and glued to a paperback book when I first noticed her. My assigned seat was next to hers, but she didn't notice me. I couldn't help but observe that she was a little different.

I wonder what nationality she is, I thought. *Maybe I can get a clue if I can see what she's reading.*

Inconspicuously, I glanced at her book. Before I knew it, I had asked, "Can you actually read that?" It looked foreign—Russian, perhaps.

She dropped the book and stated very frankly in her broken English, "No! I am just looking at the pages to impress people like you!"

I felt awful. Talking about getting off to a bad start! "I'm sorry. I hope you'll accept my apology. Of course, I know you can read it. You see, I am just impressed. I mean, I don't even speak very good English, much less any other language. I do hope you will forgive my lack of sensitivity. Let me introduce myself. I'm Marsha Spradlin."

"I'm Gabby. Well, that's not really my name, but it's what people here call me. Really, it's OK. I'm used to people staring and asking questions. It's been that way all of my life," she explained.

Puzzled, I didn't know how to respond. Should I pursue the conversation or just let her return to her book? After a moment, I realized she was waiting for me to respond.

"Oh, so you have lived here all of your life?" I asked.

"Oh, no! My life is far more complicated than that," she replied.

She was right. During the next hour and a half, she unfolded her

A Magnificent Encounter

story. I clung to every word for several reasons. First, her English was difficult to understand. And second, her story was incredible—almost like a novel.

Gabby grew up in a wealthy Russian family. Her father was a government official. His responsibilities included engineering the Amazon Dam in South America. This meant she moved to South America while still in her teens. There she first experienced rejection and prejudice. "No one accepted a Russian, especially not there, then!" she pointed out.

While in South America, political unrest broke out. Gabby's father was the target of a political conspiracy. One night, her home was vandalized, and both parents murdered. Gabby and her two younger brothers escaped.

"That was when I learned something of responsibility. I was the oldest, but still a child. Someone had to take care of my brothers. We fled for our lives as we sought refuge," she continued. How they survived the months on the run was in itself a story.

The three found a hiding place where they spent the next several years. Gabby found a job cleaning. That provided enough money to buy food and pay for a tiny shelter.

During that time, she met Frank, a military man from the United States. He was of a different race, but skin color did not matter to Gabby. In 1984 Frank's tour of duty was completed. He and Gabby had been married for six years by then and had adopted two children, one black and one white. They moved to Frank's home in San Antonio, Texas.

"Marsha, no one there wanted to be friends because we were so different. Frank's a wonderful father, and I love him and my children. But, I would love to have a friend," Gabby said.

While I did not want to miss a word, my heart was in the midst of self-examination: *Is this a coincidence? Or am I to be that friend? Am I prejudiced?* I wasn't comfortable with my answers. But I was comfortable with what I knew to be true.

Gabby wasn't only on the flight because she was scheduled to meet Frank in Atlanta. She was there because God had engineered the course of events in our lives so our hearts could touch. It wasn't a coincidence.

With Love, Marsha

It was God's plan. I had the choice of deciding how I would respond to this one seeking friendship and acceptance.

Frank had been transferred to the South. They were meeting in Atlanta to find housing and schools for the children and to make other necessary arrangements.

"We will move to the South in a month, Marsha. Will they accept us?" she asked me.

I couldn't respond. I knew the answer. Some would. Some wouldn't. At no time during our conversation did Gabby mention You, Father. I knew what I had to do. You could be the only One who could fully love and accept her and provide the friendship and refuge she was seeking.

"Gabby, I am not sure how well you and Frank will be accepted when you move. But I am sure about one thing. I do know Who can give you love and friendship, not to mention acceptance," I said.

Gabby's life of hurting, hunting, and hunger made her heart open. She clung to every word as I explained who You are and why she could trust You. Apparently, no one had ever introduced her to Jesus Christ.

The flight landed in Atlanta. I was scheduled to make connections to Birmingham. Gabby was to meet Frank. I knew we might never see each other again, but the seed of hope had been planted. But I also knew that I needed to seek Your forgiveness for prejudice I did not even know I had. It was an obstacle that could block an effective witness. My time with Gabby made me examine my own tendency to judge.

Father, I am convinced that we miss bright encounters because of fear, lack of awareness, feeling incompetent in our ability to identify with persons different from ourselves, as well as lack of availability due to prejudices.

Today's experience with Gabby was a bright but painful encounter. It is difficult to see ourselves as we really are. Help me, Father, to see how I can overcome my tendency to judge. Only when I live a life free of judgment can I demonstrate what it means to be Yours so my witness can really count.

With love,
Marsha

The Tapestry

Dear Child,

How many are your works, O Lord! In wisdom you made them all; the earth is full of your creatures.

So God created man in his own image, in the image of God he created him; male and female he created them.

When God created man, he made him in the likeness of God. He created them male and female; at the time they were created, he blessed them and called them "man."

For you created my inmost being; you knit me together in my mother's womb. I will praise you because I am fearfully and wonderfully made; your works are wonderful, I know that full well.

For we are God's workmanship; created in Christ Jesus to do good works, which God prepared in advance for us to do.

To be made new in the attitude of your minds; and to put on the new self, created to be like God in true righteousness and holiness.

For by him all things were created: things in heaven and on earth, visible and invisible, whether thrones or powers or rulers or authorities; all things were created by him and for him.

For everything God created is good, and nothing is to be rejected if it is received with thanksgiving, because it is consecrated by the word of God and prayer.

Your Father
(Ps. 104:24; Gen. 1:27; 5:1-2; Ps. 139:13-14; Eph. 2:10; 4:24; Col. 1:16; 1 Tim. 4:4)

With Love, Marsha

Dear Father:

The knock on the front door was not expected. Neither was the guest. I swung back the door as he stood in the doorway, plunging the gift into my hands.

"Happy birthday!" he greeted me. "For you, handmade. I picked out the colors myself. Then, I watched them make it. Hurry! Open it. I know it's months until your birthday—I will consider this an advance?"

My unexpected guest was an old friend from college, Jack. He had just returned from a three-week trip to India. He had a layover in my city and decided to make the surprise visit.

I hugged him as he entered my apartment. The gift was heavy. The box was round. My curiosity grew as I quickly removed the ribbon, tape, and protective wrapping.

Slowly, I unrolled it. The gift was an original tapestry. It was meant to be used as a rug, yet I would not dare step on such a piece of art. The colors matched my apartment perfectly. I was thrilled with the breathtaking beauty.

I put on a pot of coffee while Jack explained the process of having the rug designed. He related in minute detail how he selected the individual threads and design, met the weaver, and watched each inch of it as it was formed. He was most impressed with the final stage—the molding of the tapestry. With tiny scissors the weaver cut each thread as if to make a sculpture. It was a sculptured tapestry—a treasure.

For years, the tapestry has been in the center of my living room. I have enjoyed telling new friends of its origin. Each time I share the story of the gift, I think about You, Father.

Father, my life is a thread in Your tapestry. Your hand has carefully woven my life into part of Your master design. My life has been interwoven—into the woof and warp—and intertwined with the lives of my brothers and sisters. We each become colors and have a part to play in Your tapestry. Through joy and pain You use our experiences to add texture to Your design of love, and together we can make the fabric strong and spiritually exquisite.

I cannot always see the pattern, Father. We, the fabric, are a collection of people as diverse as the cells in our bodies. As my life crosses patterns with others, Your fabric starts to grow. And when You are finished, an exquisite creation can be seen for all the world to enjoy.

83
The Tapestry

Yet, You will still know every thread by name, for no two threads mean the same in Your everlasting tapestry.

May I continue to seek Your creative hand in my life, Father. After all, You have chosen me to be a thread in Your tapestry of life. On occasions sabering doubts inside of me rumble. You have chosen me? But over the years, I have learned and been humbled as I find You in the faces of my fellow Christians—each almost shockingly different from me, each adding strength to the fabric. Therefore, the basis of our unity is found not within our similarity but in our diversity, colors, skills, abilities, and gifts. No wonder cynics have looked at the body and sighed, "Are these the people who represent God?"

May my life be a tapestry that others will recognize as being custom designed by You. Continue to weave me into Your design. Stitch my life by removing the excess from Your design. Then, may this tapestry not only be a centerpiece marked by the beauty woven by You, but one that is sincerely used for You.

With love,
Marsha

PART 3:
Your Mysteries

"There is a God in heaven that reveals secrets" (Dan. 2:28).

The Mystery of Your Magnificence

Dear Child:

Can you fathom the mysteries of God? Can you probe the limits of the Almighty? They are higher than the heavens—what can you do? They are deeper than the depths of the grave—what can you know? Their measure is longer than the earth and wider than the sea.

If I have the gift of prophecy and can fathom all mysteries and all knowledge, and if I have a faith that can move mountains, but have not love, I am nothing.

Surely you have heard about the administration of God's grace that was given to me for you, that is, the mystery made known to me by revelation. Although I am less than the least of all God's people, this grace was given me: to preach to the Gentiles the unsearchable riches of Christ, and to make plain to everyone the administration of this mystery, which for ages past was kept hidden in God, who created all things.

My purpose is that they may be encouraged in heart and united in love, so that they may have the full riches of complete understanding in order that they may know the mystery of God, namely Christ, in whom are hidden the treasures of wisdom and knowledge.

Your Father
(Job 11:7-9; 1 Cor. 13:2; Eph. 3:2-3,8-9; Col. 2:2-3)

With Love, Marsha

Dear Father:

It took every ounce of energy I had to push open the front door. Then I stood in wonder. The hush was too silent to describe. I was surrounded by a "winter wonderland."

"Snow?" I screamed. This was not expected, not on April 15. After standing nearly knee-deep in white disbelief for several minutes, I ran into my office to grab a ruler. *I must measure this. No one will believe we have this much snow in mid April*, I thought.

I dropped the ruler into the pile of white fluff outside the front door. Eight inches! Incredible! You continue to fascinate me, Father. This is an unexpected surprise. My fascination was interrupted by my telephone. The call was from my supervisor. "It's a snow day!" she chirped with excitement. "The office is closed. Stay home!"

I probably should have spent the day working, but I positively couldn't. I pulled the winter clothes (which I had just stored for the season) from my closet. After covering my body with layers of wool, I fetched the camera. I wanted to capture this mystery, to keep this April snow forever.

As I walked through the backyard, I felt the snow crunch under my feet. The neighborhood children were making a snowman. Almost as strange as snow in April was the fact that I was not cold. That, too, was a mystery. Maybe I was focusing my attention so fully on snapping pictures that I was unaware of the temperature.

The longer I stayed outside, the more questions I had about the mysteries of this unusual phenomenon. Is it true that no two snowflakes are alike? I'd prove the answer if I could succeed in finding two identical flakes. *What do I know about snowflakes?* I thought.

After an hour, my toes began to lose their feeling. I decided to go inside for hot chocolate to satisfy my body. To satisfy my curiosity, I tried to find my copy of *The Old Farmer's Almanac*. I had remembered reading something about snowflakes in the 1986 edition. Finding it in my study, embedded among hundreds of books, was almost as challenging as finding two identical snowflakes.

Finding it wasn't nearly as thrilling as what I found tucked inside its pages. I learned that a single crystal of snow weighs only a millionth of a gram. A cup of snow contains more than 10 million flakes. Someone has estimated that 100,000,000,000,000,000,000,000,000 snowflakes fall on

89
The Mystery of Your Magnificence

New England in a typical snowstorm. Is it really possible out of that unimaginable large number, no two are alike? My almanac had the answer. It introduced the intriguing 1865 research of Wilson Bentley who explored the odds of duplication. During the span of his life, Bentley had accumulated nearly 5,000 microphotographs of the six-sided snow crystal. He won worldwide fame as an expert on the meteorology of snow. It was written of Bentley, "He saw something in the snowflakes which other men failed to see, not because they could not see, but because they had not the patience and the understanding to look." We have Bentley's word. There is a simple but mind-boggling mathematical explanation that answers this question—sort of.

Bentley saw in the simple snowflake one of nature's deepest mysteries. To Bentley, the snowflake exemplified the kaleidoscopic balance of order and disorder. That is the basis of beauty in art and nature.

Why am I so enchanted with the mystery of the snowflake? I see a parallel, Father. In one sense, no two snowflakes are alike; yet in another sense, all snowflakes are alike. The diversity is a measure of nature's potential for chance. The constancy of the snowflake's six-sided form reassures me that nature is ruled by law.

Father, I am a snowflake. Truly, I am. There is no one like me. That is even a greater mystery. Look at my hands. They are remarkable. They are rare. Marvelous. No one has hands exactly like mine. And my eyes. Father, You have placed inside them millions of receptors with which to see the snow as it falls and the seasons as they change. Look at my ears. I can hear the snow crunch beneath my feet. And a voice! My voice can encourage those who are depressed and affirm those who feel abused. No one has a voice exactly like mine. And my body. You did not condemn me to stand straight without movement like a tree frozen in a mid-April snowstorm. I can move quickly. I can throw a snowball. I can reach out and love. I can touch the hurting. I can move forward! Inside me, You have designed 500 muscles, 200 bones, and 700 miles of nerves—all perfectly synchronized by You! There is no one else like me. In all the years of history, You have created only one me! I am unique and rare.

Like snowflakes, no two persons are alike; in another sense, all people are alike. The diversity in humanity is Your way to demonstrate Your

With Love, Marsha

magnificence. Yet your consistency shows as you make human beings in Your image.

Today has been a magnificent day—one I shall hold onto. Once again, You have taught as I apply Your letters to my day. Like Bentley's view of the snowflake, You see in me something others may fail to see. It's not because they cannot see; they just don't have the patience and understanding to look. You see potential in me!

I am reminded of the farm folks in the north who dread the winter. Many think of snow as slush and snow chains. But I want to see it for what it is—a mystery. May it continually remind me of the way Your beauty arises from a delicate balance of law, chaos, and change. Likewise, may it continue to teach me that You command me not to walk as my brother or talk as my leader. You don't want me to be anything but myself. You have called me to show my rarity to the world. Your letters challenge me not to conform any longer to the patterns of the world, but to be transformed! Yes, Father. I am wonderfully made. May I acknowledge the mystery of my magnificence by being Your body, Your hands, Your feet, and Your voice. I am Yours! Let it snow!

With love,
Marsha

The Cornerstone

Dear Child:
 See, I lay a stone in Zion, a tested stone, a precious cornerstone for a sure foundation; the one who trusts will never be dismayed. In the beginning you laid the foundations of the earth, and the heavens are the works of your hands.
 By the grace God has given me, I laid a foundation as an expert builder, and someone else is building on it. But each one should be careful how he builds. For no one can lay any foundation other than the one already laid, which is Jesus Christ.

Your Father
(Isa. 28:16; Ps. 102:25; 1 Cor. 3:10-11)

With Love, Marsha

Dear Father:

Today I had a thrilling experience. Thank you for the opportunity to revisit my childhood. I enjoyed each moment at the old farm where my grandparents once lived. I have exciting memories of hot days spent there with my grandparents and the farm animals.

While it was fun to go back, I was rather disappointed. I guess it is not uncommon to feel a letdown—things were certainly not the same. The house was not as large as I remembered it. The trees surely were not as tall. Had they changed?

Nothing actually had changed. In reality, the house and trees were the same. Perhaps I was different. My perspective had changed. As I grew, my world grew as well. Those good old summer days were a positive foundation—cornerstone experiences on which to build many more experiences.

While I had fun revisiting the past, I knew I could not stay there. Because I have grown since childhood, I am not satisfied to spend every day playing at the farm. My priorities have changed, and my definition of fun does not include playing with farm animals.

My visit to the past today taught me three truths. Father, help me apply all three to my relationship with You, as well as my relationships with my church and friends.

First, I learned that my early farm experiences served as a foundation on which to build and continue to grow. Likewise, my early spiritual experiences serve the same beneficial purpose. They afford building and growing. My relationship to You and my church must continue to play an important part in maintaining that secure foundation.

Second, my life is different. My perspective has changed—it is more inclusive. My life now is different from my life as a non-Christian. As I have grown spiritually, I want to reach out to more people—even people who may be vastly different from me.

Third, I cannot go back to the way it was; I must move forward. I must continue to grow, expand, and reach out. I know too much to be satisfied with life as it was. My knowledge of You and Your mandate to tell the world of Christ's love has made me want to move forward with Your love. I want to continue to grow in my knowledge of You. I want to expand and reach out to those who are hurting. If not me, then who? If not now, then when? If not for Christ, why? If not with my gifts, with

93
The Cornerstone

what? If not in my own neighborhood, where? If not through You, how?

Father, yesterday is but a dream and tomorrow only a vision, but today, well lived, makes every yesterday a dream of Christian joy and every tomorrow a vision of hope. Help me look well into this day. May this be the foundational salutation inscribed in the cornerstone of my life. Let me not cease from exploring my past. But, as I explore, teach me Your true knowledge. Perhaps in the end of all my exploring, I will arrive where I started but will know that place for the first time.

So, kind Father, help me realize that it is not how much I have or the accumulation of my life's experiences but how much I enjoy recognizing cornerstone experiences that yield spiritual joy and genuine security. It's not arriving at the end of life's journey of cornerstone experiences that makes life abundant; it is the joy of the journey. So, grant this day serenity for today's journey. Lead me to recognize cornerstone experiences of today that will be a foundation for tomorrow.

With love,
Marsha

A Time to Grow

Dear Child:
   See how the lilies of the fields grow. They do not labor or spin.
   But grow in the grace and knowledge of our Lord and Savior Jesus Christ. To him be glory both now and forever!

Your Father
(Matt. 6:28; 2 Pet. 3:18)

A Time to Grow

Dear Father:

After opening my car door, Christopher quickly smiled and reached for my hand. He wrapped his arms tightly around me and said, "I love you."

I looked at his radiant blue eyes and thought, *Could this be the same little boy who I held tightly in my arms just a few years ago? Look at him! He is taller than his daddy and so confident.*

He reached into his pocket and pulled out a gold key chain. "My birthday present," he said with a smile stretched across his typical teenage face. "Keys to the car. I got my driver's license today!"

"Christopher, when did you suddenly grow so tall? I was home only two months ago. Where is my baby nephew?" I asked.

"I don't know, Aunt Marsha, but I would like to borrow your car. Can I?" he asked.

Who could possibly say no to this birthday king with the blue eyes? "Certainly—but keep it in between the ditches. It is nearly paid for," I explained.

For a brief moment, my thoughts traveled to another bright birthday encounter with this young man. He was indeed young, then. It was his third birthday, and I had promised him a trip to the beach.

Early that special morning, I picked up Christopher, his sand bucket, towel, an extra set of clothes, and a picnic basket. In moments, we were off for a joyful day—just the two of us—to explore the beach at Gulf Shores. During the one-hour drive, he continued to ask, "How much farther, Aunt Marsha?"

"Not much farther," I replied.

Within moments, he asked the question again and again, until we finally arrived. I was amazed at his lack of sense of time. Five minutes meant nothing to him. His only concern was getting there.

In a noble attempt to divert his attention, I tried to explain what he would see at the beach. As an adult talks to a three-year-old, I described the sand.

"How much sand will there be?" he asked.

His questions were difficult. I used the "change-the-subject" method and tried to describe the water.

"How much water will there be? And how much longer until we get to the beach, Aunt Marsha?" he asked.

With Love, Marsha

One hour seemed like eternity to Christopher. As soon as I unloaded him and the beach equipment, we walked hand in hand, barefoot, over the hot sand. Soon we were there. It was a priceless moment. Christopher stood quietly and simply looked at the sand. He stared into the infinite sea. I said nothing. Two or three minutes passed. Finally, his brilliant blue eyes focused on me. He pulled my hand. He wanted to be held. I dropped the bucket, towels, and basket and gently took him in my arms. He wrapped his arms around my shoulders and said, "I love you, all the way to the beach and back." I cherish the memory and the simplicity of Christopher's description of love.

Father, could this be the same little boy? While years have helped him grow taller and more intellectually articulate, I know he still loves me all the way to the beach and back. His growth has just taught him to say better what he means. But his love could not grow any bigger than it was that moment when he first compared it to his perspective of the infinite distance to the beach.

What is growth? Can it always be measured? Christopher's physical growth is easy to measure. Yet, can spiritual growth be measured as easily? I think of Christopher's childlike sensitivity and openness in expressing love. Perhaps my spiritual growth can only be measured by my growing more sensitive to others. May I always have the ability to hear beyond the words that are spoken and see beyond the obvious.

Like the sand on which we stood years ago, I can only grow as I build on a foundation. Such building does not often come in spurts like an adolescent boy. It is most often a consistent building, daily. Regardless of the consistency, it is the foundation that counts. If I build to please myself, I am building on the sand. Yet, if I build to demonstrate my love for You, I am building on solid rock.

One day Christopher will reach the limit of his physical growth. Unlike physical growth which is limited, there is plenty of room to grow spiritually. There is room for my intellect to grow in knowledge of You. There is room for my heart to grow in caring for others. There is room for my feet to grow in relationships. There is plenty of growing room for every phase of my spiritual growth, but I will grow spiritually only as I make room for You. And just as Christopher gazed at the sea and sand and saw infinity, I make room for you in my outlook—my chosen perspective about everything.

A Time to Grow

Father, growth for me has sometimes been difficult. I do believe I have had my share of growing pains. I love what you said about the lilies. "Consider the lilies of the field, how they grow" (Matt. 6:28, KJV). Once again, your words have taught me about growth. A lily is not always in the sunshine; for the greater part of the year, it is hidden in the earth. How does it grow? Lilies grow in the dark. Only for a short time are they radiantly beautiful and sweet. I can never be a lily in the garden unless I have spent time as a bulb in the dark, totally ignored. That is how I grow.

Teach me to grow. Give me patience to grow in darkness. Only then can I capture the full radiant beauty and meaning of the sunshine moments at the beach when I am told "I love you all the way to the beach and back." May I continue to grow.

With love,
Marsha

Warm and Wonderfully Made

Dear Child:
 I tell you the truth, unless you change and become like little children, you will never enter the kingdom of heaven. Therefore, whoever humbles himself like this is the greatest in the kingdom of heaven.
 Every good and perfect gift is from above coming down from the Father of the heavenly lights, who does not change like shifting shadows.

Your Father
(Matt. 18:3; Jas. 1:17)

Warm and Wonderfully Made

Dear Father:

As I drove to work this morning, I sensed the change. The once-green foliage is now a montage of amber, rust, purple, and yellow. I noticed fewer leaves on the trees; one by one they have relinquished their branches. The visible change appears to be death. The trees are dying. Yet, I remember enough biology to recognize that this change is a result of a deeper change within nature. It is a visible statement that winter will soon envelop this mountain range. The trees are preparing for the cold. They are releasing their foliage to embrace the storm and prepare for new life.

It's strikingly beautiful—the change, that is. Never have I seen the mountain so brilliant. But why do I always think of *change* as a stark or even cold or harsh word? Often I am afraid and even panic because my deepest desire is to keep things just as they are. I have never really respected change for its positive value. Maybe I need to become like a child to learn and appreciate Your many great wonders and mysteries of life and death.

Speaking of children, I loved the inspirational allegory illustrating the delicate balance between life and death in the book *The Fall of Freddie the Leaf*. It helped me understand how Freddie and his companion leaves changed with the passing seasons, finally falling to the ground with winter's snow. As Freddie landed on a clump of snow,

> It somehow felt soft and even warm. In this new position he was more comfortable than he had ever been. He closed his eyes and fell asleep. He did not know that Spring would follow Winter and that the snow would melt into water. He did not know that what appeared to be his useless dried self would join with the water and serve to make the tree stronger. Most of all, he did not know that there, asleep in the tree and the ground, were already plans for new leaves in the Spring.[1]

The fall was really the beginning.

Change is such a warm and wonderfully wise work of Your beginnings. Change is perhaps the most consistent part of my life. It is personal, and it is everywhere—like the air we breathe. There couldn't be life like we know it without change. Yet, just when we begin to experience what I call security, we often notice change creeping in and gently whispering, "It's time to let go."

100
With Love, Marsha

Most often the winds of change move in gently, like the expected change of the seasons each year. It is not unlike the earth I walk on. Even it shifts continuously with change. To live is to change. Sometimes I choose it. Sometimes it is forced on me. Sometimes new things are exchanged for old things. Other times things look different than before. Sometimes change happens because something is lost. The loss can be slight or a transformation of one's life. Change can be, I feel, one of the most delightful miracles as I let go of the person I am now, only to merge with the person I am to become. My life becomes a process of becoming, and becoming means changing.

Father, if change is so natural and a part of Your plan, why am I so inclined to hold onto the security and comfortable certainties of my past rather than take on the uncertainties of the future You have planned for me? The choice to change is mine. To live is to change. I do want to participate fully in living, Father, and I can collaborate in the shaping of my life by listening to Your voice. I can choose Your change and let it shape me into a magnificent mold You have created me to be. Or, I can become a victim of it and shaped unwillingly by it—a mold easily broken and prone to crumbling and deterioration.

I remember distinctly the last major change of my life. It was leaving a secure job and moving 650 miles to begin a new job and life experience. During those months of adjustment, the changes bombarded me from every direction. I felt grief as I let go of my past securities and successes. But growth followed. Sure, there were days of adjustments. I had a different home, church, office, bank, driver's license number, grocery store, phone number, office procedure, ad infinitum. But, as I adjusted to my new environment, I recognized that change had summoned me to a deeper level of challenge, creativity, courage, and commitment. The results were a deeper discovery of who I am. Thank You for change.

Like Freddie, may I always be open to Your changes. Teach me to view change as a positive force in my life, suggesting that I let go, but yielding to growth. I choose to change.

With love,
Marsha

101
Warm and Wonderfully Made
Note

1. Leo Buscaglia, *The Fall of Freddie the Leaf* (New York: Charles B. Slack, Inc., 1982).

Going Home

Dear Child:

Like a bird that strays from its nest is a man who strays from his home.

Foxes have holes and birds of the air have nests, but the Son of Man has no place to lay his head.

Your Father
(Prov. 2:7-8; Matt. 8:20)

Going Home

Dear Father:

Autumn is here. The signs are everywhere. The leaves are changing, dropping, and sweeping across my front lawn. The overhead dramas of flocks of birds traveling south amaze me. Their instinct commands the time to fly in strategic formations. They live by no tangible clock or calendar that tells them the time or date. Yet, they know.

I have been watching birds for days now. Those traveling south seem countless. I have wondered where they are coming from and how far they have already traveled.

I must be one of Your most curious children. My questions about the laws of nature almost seem as endless as the number of birds flying over my house.

To satisfy my hunger to know, I bought a bird book. I spent hours last night glued to the pages. I was so intrigued to learn of the many species of birds. Each has a unique set of incredible characteristics. I had not realized how many of those characteristics apply to the "birds" I am around. Some birds even seem to imitate my own life.

Canadian geese flying in a V-shape afford one example. As I understand it, there is not one lead goose. Aerodynamic specialists insist that geese can fly enormous distances only because each goose helps the flock by taking its turn as leader. Leadership is rotated because no goose can stay up front forever.

Geese stick together. Fast ones are usually up front and weak ones fly on the sides. When one falls away, other geese break away from the "V" to lead the departed goose back to the formation. However, it would not take the stray goose very long to realize how much he missed the crowd. Flying alone is more difficult because of the lack of the wind tunnel produced by the "V." The smart goose speeds up and flies back in line as fast as possible.

My bird book described what happens to geese in the formation wind tunnel. In flapping its own wings, each goose creates an upward lift for the following goose. The result is a 71 percent greater flying range than if each goose flew alone!

Father, how often have I been a goose? Leadership does take its toll. I must admit, I cannot stay in front forever. I need time to rest and others need opportunities to lead. By rotating responsibility, we begin to build on each other's strengths and weaknesses. We extend the range of our effectiveness. No longer do I need to feel that I must hide my weaknesses. For in my weakness, I realize Your strength. Help me, Father, to learn from the geese. When others fall behind, may I not be so focused on being the leader that I fail to break away to encourage the stray goose to merge back into the formation You have designed.

The turkey was most intriguing. Turkeys are really considered lazy. Their main goal is eating. The result is they are eaten. Because they eat so much, they are unable to fly. They are grounded. Their wings just cannot support their weight. They are self-centered.

May I not be a turkey or run around with "turkeys." May I not become so obsessed with feeding myself, even spiritually, that I fail to exercise my wings. May I never be grounded because I cannot support my own weight. It is possible to spend so much time studying, reading, thinking, writing, and analyzing that I fail to apply what I have learned.

While I do like turkey, literally, let me never be guilty of imitating those whose lives are characteristic of this self-centered bird. Instead, let me encourage them as I emulate a life free from self-centeredness.

Hummingbirds are my favorite. I identify with them more than any other. I have had opportunities to observe the tiny hummingbird flap its tiny wings at the rate of sixty miles per hour while remaining still. It occurred to me that it takes as much energy to remain in one place as it does to soar. How often, Father, have I been guilty of flapping my wings as hard as I could without going anywhere. The reason is obvious—I was flapping in my own strength. Let me never be guilty of only flapping my wings. My energy alone will take me nowhere. Only when I yield my entire being to You can You put my life's energy into motion.

Because of *Jonathan Livingston Seagull*, I had some background knowledge of the sea gull. But I was not prepared for the negative implication of my findings. Father, I did not know that sea gulls ate trash. They are independent birds—wanting to do their own thing. They ostracize birds that are different, even other sea gulls. As soon as one sea gull falters, the others pounce upon him. If a sea gull ever falls away, he is out forever. I do not sense a forgiving, loving spirit in the sea gull family.

How often have I wanted to be the independent one in my family—wanting to do my own thing—regardless of the price? How often have I let my spiritual, mental, emotional, and physical self go down the drain

Going Home

simply because I ate trash? I firmly believe I am what I eat, as well as what I read. Teach me, Father, to drink Your living water; read Your letters; think loving thoughts; and take care of the temple You have given me by resting, eating properly, and exercising. May I never be guilty of exercising a critical spirit that condemns and ostracizes those who are different. That is prejudice. And when I see one lagging behind and drifting from the pattern, may I again be like the goose—quick to encourage and escort him or her back to the flock.

Thank You for giving me sight to see the birds soaring. Thank You for ears to hear their melodies. Thank You for a heart that can learn from these delicate, yet majestic, creatures. They can be my teachers. May my life soar with a song as sweet and sincere as the birds in my own backyard.

With love,
Marsha

A Voice in the Wind

Dear Child:
 The wind blows wherever it pleases. You hear its sound, but you cannot tell where it comes from or where it is going. So it is with everyone born of the Spirit.
 He makes winds his messengers, flames of fire his servants.

Your Father
(John 3:8; Ps. 104:4)

107
A Voice in the Wind

Dear Father:

The wind is blowing hard right now. The air is brisk. It's time to pull out sweaters and jackets, but winter is still weeks away. The cold wind is unexpected and premature.

Only a few days ago, I was here at the lake with several friends. We enjoyed the day riding bicycles underneath the steady stream of sunbeams. I can still hear the crowds of friendly, carefree picnic parties, chasing Frisbees, grilling hamburgers, and seeing couples walking hand in hand.

I almost feel pain when I compare now with then. Any moment, these clouds will break open, and rain will spill into the lake. This once-crowded park will become quiet. The storm will surround a solitude. It will be an isolated island reserved for those wishing to catch a glimpse of a different kind of beauty. It can only be captured by those who wish to pay the price of enduring wind and rain. That means wind-blown hair and an additional three pounds of weight due to soaked jeans and sweatshirts.

It's hard to write—the wind is blowing that hard. My notebook wants to escape the picnic table planted underneath this abandoned oak tree. But I really do not feel a need to write. Instead, I need to listen to Your voice.

It is now late. I have spent most of the morning sitting, listening, and watching Your voice and action in the wind, before I joined the ranks of escapists forced to break for shelter. It was an enchanting experience to hear and see Your voice through the wind. As I clung to the cold, concrete picnic table, I watched sailboats maneuver over the mysterious waves. Each was tossed by the force. How strange it was that each boat was going in a different direction within the same body of water. Yet, each was powered by the same source—the wind. I could barely see the sailboats being tossed about. I could not see the source of their power. I could only feel its effects. At times, my tiny body was almost lifted off the table by the sudden gusts of wind.

As I observed the boats, I realized that most of the sailors probably could not explain how it all worked—the power and the sails. Nor could they predict when the powerful source of energy would again be available. Each sailor was required to wait. None of them needed to seek the power. The wind does not reward those who are too anxious or impatient. To seek it shows not only impatience and greed but also lack of faith. Your voice in the wind, Father, can teach me patience and faith, if I am willing to ride out the storm.

As I watched the wind treat each sailor equally, I realized that its power was available to all. The sailor made the difference. Each sailor just had to wait for the wind—some waited patiently, while others were impatient. Their responses spoke volumes. Some were not prepared and were caught with their sails down, missing their chance to take advantage of the powerful wind. Some were so frightened by the sudden surge of the wind's force that they froze and missed the opportunity to move forward. Some were stricken—their boats toppled over and nearly sank. Some struggled to learn how to maneuver the sail—they appeared to be inexperienced sailors yet willing to learn, even though learning meant taking chances. Perhaps these were those who eventually become "real" sailors. Finally, some were fully prepared—accomplished, seasoned sailors. They could move forward with the same source of power that had devastated, frustrated, and sunk fellow sailors around them.

What did it all mean—the voices in the wind? Maybe, I, too, could use the power from this unseen and mysterious source during the unexpected storms and even frightening periods of my life.

Father, could I use this power—the wind—to work for me when life seems to sabotage me? Can I gain power from this force that I have been interpreting as negative to make some experiences positive? Even failure? Father, could I be so brave as to look directly into the wind's intimidating face and sail forward? Is it really up to me to choose how I will use the invisible, mysterious power?

How will I choose to use the wind? Will I choose to be frightened, overcome, frustrated, and even caught off guard? All of these responses can make me topple over or even sink. Will I wait patiently, sitting tightly in my little boat listening for Your voice in the wind and trusting that at the perfect moment I can move forward?

I must be prepared and make myself ready. I must be willing to wait. I must demonstrate patience. I must be willing to learn. Likewise, I must be willing nearly to sink. Father, I must know that I can always climb back into the boat and try again if I fail. Sooner or later, I will learn how to use the wind and its power.

Father, is it true that when the wind is blowing the hardest I have the

A Voice in the Wind

ability to move the greatest distance? I choose to recognize the voice as it is meant to be heard. Only I can decide how I will set my sails. Maybe I should consider sailing school! Will you teach me to listen to Your voice in the wind?

With love,
Marsha

* Thanks to Broadman Press for allowing me to adapt "A Voice in the Wind" from my Broadman book, *Transformed One Winter* (Nashville: Broadman Press, 1989).

Who's Who

Dear Child:
Your attitude should be the same as that of Christ Jesus. . . . taking the very nature of a servant. . . . he humbled himself and became obedient.

For those God foreknew he also predestined to be conformed to the likeness of his Son, that he might be the firstborn among many brothers.

Let us make man in our image, in our likeness.

Your Father
(Phil. 2:5,7-8; Rom. 8:29; Gen. 1:26)

Who's Who?

Dear Father:

The Christmas season triggers so many emotions. Instead of the focus being on You, it has often been inundated with artificial tinsel and ribbon. Yet, I cherish the bringing together of friends and family. Last night's Christmas party was more than a special gathering of friends. It was a time of sharing, listening, and loving one another. The hostess asked each of us to share a Christmas memory. As I listened to my friends, I was amazed at the variety, yet similarity, of experiences. Each story was different. But the common theme was that each memory shared centered on a childhood experience. In my case, I told the story of Justin, my three-year-old nephew.

It was Christmas Eve two years before. As is the custom of the Spradlin family, we gathered in the living room to enjoy a family celebration. The hour was very late. My brother, Larry, excused himself to put Justin into bed. As we overheard the conversation between Larry and Justin, we made a mental note of Larry's final instructions: "Justin, I had better not see you out of that bed." Larry rejoined the family as we discussed how long it would be until Justin thought of a legitimate excuse to crawl out of bed. After five minutes, Justin walked bravely into the living room and announced: "Daddy, this is not me you see."

Justin's clever and creative technique to camouflage himself worked. For several moments, we were laughing so hard we couldn't see anything. Justin's imagination had defined what was real. By changing his perspective of himself, he was convinced that he could also change ours.

This experience, hilarious as it was, made me consider deeply the implications of the Christmas as well as Christian camouflage. How often have I failed to make Christ known because of my own camouflage, regardless of the season? How often have I allowed the season of Christmas to be camouflaged beyond recognition? Perhaps others have felt as I have that "this isn't really Christ that we see in Christmas."

Father, challenge me to redefine my Christian identity as well as the meaning of the season. When others look at me, do they see You or see me? During this special time of year, do I celebrate Your life in me, or do I celebrate activity? May others say, "That is indeed Christ I see."

With love,
Marsha

A Spring Cleaning

Dear Child:

Wash away all my iniquity and cleanse me from my sin. Cleanse me with hyssop, and I will be clean; wash me, and I will be whiter than snow.

He who has clean hands and a pure heart. . . . He will receive blessing from the Lord and vindication from God his Savior.

"I will return to the house I left" . . . swept clean and put in order.

First clean the inside of the cup and dish, and then the outside also will be clean.

You are already clean because of the word I have spoken to you. Remain in me, and I will remain in you.

If a man cleanses himself from the latter, he will be an instrument for noble purpose, made holy, useful to the Master and prepared to do any good work.

Your Father
(Pss. 51:2,7; 24:4-5; Matt. 12:44; 23:26; John 15:3-4; 2 Tim. 2:21)

113
A Spring Cleaning

Dear Father:

I couldn't stand the filth any longer. How the spring pollen finds its way into my house is one of nature's most phenomenal mysteries. Yet, today's spring cleaning wasn't only removing dust. It included ridding the house of the piles that had accumulated over the past weeks, months, and even year! I had hid most of it well, but I had known all along it was there. I felt repelled by both the unorganized clutter and the effort it would take to clean and organize my house. But I couldn't put off cleaning another second. It had to be done.

The first question I faced was, "Where do I begin?" I felt the need to break the cleaning process into phases. The first phase was cleaning the obvious—big boulders like the pile of laundry, the stacks of papers in the corner of the office—getting rid of what was not needed to make room for what was needed. That included going through the closets and old magazines. This phase went fast. But when the boulders were gone, I began to spy out a veritable collection of smaller rocks that had to be cleared away. When those were gone, I noticed a multitude of stones and tiny pebbles I had not seen before. This was the hardest and most tedious work. But I stuck to it. Finally, by the end of the day, my house was clean.

That cleaning experience reminds me so much of my private, spiritual world. When I first became a Christian, I was serious about blasting away the boulders—the major sins that had become habits and had collected in my life. Lord, You pointed out many major behaviors that needed to be altered and removed. As the years have passed, many of those giant boulders have been demolished by the Holy Spirit's dynamite. Habits that used to be so hard to break are no longer present. Instead, I do know peace and freedom.

Yet, as major habits or boulders have disappeared, I have discovered another layer of actions and attitudes I had not seen before. Father, You saw them. One by one You rebuked them. This process was lengthy and exhausting, but it was carried out. Then, when I reached the point in my Christian life where You and I were dealing with stones and pebbles, I began to realize they were too numerous to imagine. I felt we would be dealing with pebbles for the rest of my life. Each day, part of my spiritual cleaning must include the discipline of cleaning away the pebbles.

With Love, Marsha

The process isn't as simple as I thought. Boulders can even reappear in my house if I don't give special attention to cleaning each day. As I become caught up in my daily routine, these boulders, stones, and pebbles can begin to collect and roll back into the corners and closets of my life. They can hide beneath the surface, but eventually they will work their way up. So, one by one, with the Holy Spirit's cleansing, I will have to dispose of them.

Some boulders, rocks, and pebbles are a frustration. They appear easy to remove until I try. Only then do I discover that there is more to removing these than meets the eye. I need Your strength and power. Many are too heavy for me to lift. I feel I understand why Paul called himself "chief of sinners." Even while in jail, he was still removing pebbles and boulders. It is a lifelong process.

While all of this seems negative, I must admit I am glad I can at least recognize these impediments. May I never lose sight of the sin in my life. May it constantly nag me until I stop and have a full-scale cleaning. But I don't need to wait until spring. It's so much easier if I take care of it daily. If I ignore daily confession as part of my spiritual discipline, I will soon be overwhelmed again by the task of cleaning. I will once again have to ask, "Where do I start?"

Father, may my body be Your temple. May I continue to give attention to cultivating and cleaning it. Otherwise, it will become infested again with the sort of growth that makes it unacceptable for Your habitation. Will You be my source of strength and direction that keeps me removing the boulders, rocks, and pebbles? By taking actions daily, I demonstrate my willingness to be conformed to the image of your dear Son.

With love,
Marsha

The Imitator

Dear Child:

Be imitators of God, therefore, as dearly loved children and live a life of love, just as Christ loved and gave himself up for us as a fragrant offering and sacrifice to God.

Take my yoke upon you and learn from me, for I am gentle and humble in heart, and you will find rest for your souls. For my yoke is easy and my burden is light.

A wise son heeds his father's instruction, but a mocker does not listen to rebuke.

Your Father
(Eph. 5:1; Matt. 11:29-30; Prov. 13:1)

With Love, Marsha

Dear Father:

The tapping on the glass window did not seem to disturb him. Neither did the rows of unfamiliar faces—each pressed to the window. He was only hours old when we enthusiastically gathered to take our first peek of Mary Ann and Walter's new baby boy, Andrew. I am certain he would have been amused if he could have heard or understood the typical comments of his new friends and relatives: "He has his mother's mouth. I think he looks just like his daddy."

Imagine the potential packed into that tiny baby boy's body, I thought.

More than two years have passed since we stood outside the hospital nursery window gazing at Andrew. I have enjoyed each opportunity of watching him grow, explore his world, and discover himself. Father, he is still so tiny, but he does have his mother's mouth, and he still looks like his daddy. But he is also starting to look just like *Andrew*. He is establishing his own identity as a real person. He is becoming a little boy.

Father, as Andrew grows and recognizes his potential, he will take on other characteristics similar to Mary Ann and Walter. Soon I may observe that he walks like his daddy and has his mother's positive outlook on life. These are formative years for Andrew—years in which physical characteristics are developed as well, as important attitudes and concepts formed.

Today Mary Ann and I had lunch. I loved hearing her accounts about Andrew. "One day I would love to write a book for Andrew. I could call it *All the Things I Would Like for Andrew to Know About God*," she mused. I questioned Mary Ann to discover exactly what she felt was important for him to learn. She sort of spelled out what she wanted him to know:

- that God wants us to know *Him* personally, intimately, and joyfully—not just know *about* Him.
- that God is *completely* faithful in every situation.
- that God is active in our daily lives—in the big and the small things— and He delights in revealing Himself to people.
- that God loves—Andrew, people Andrew knows, and every person in the world.
- that we can hear His voice speaking to us deep down in our hearts.
- that He rewards obedience that comes from a love relationship

The Imitator

with Him but is grieved when we try to please Him with a "performance."

As Mary Ann and I concluded our conversation today, we agreed that her writing such a book could be a good experience. But simply writing it or even reading it to Andrew would not cause him to learn any of these important truths about You, Father. Andrew will learn about You in many of the same ways he will learn to walk like Walter. He will discover through observation, experiences, and spending time with you.

Most of my learning from You and about You has come by spending quality time with You. You are the Master Teacher.

Father, I want to learn of You. I want to learn from You. Unfortunately, I cannot do this by reading Your letters alone, nor by reading books on all of the truths I need to know about You. I will learn of You by observing the work of Your hands in my life and the lives of others; experiencing you in my everyday life; and living with You day by day, moment by moment.

Father, how much of You do I really know from observation, experiences, and personal encounters with You as we live together? Doesn't that knowledge become real only when it results in some type of change? What changes have been made in my life this year? This month? Today?

Teach me, Father. Guide my learning in the trite, everyday moments as well as in the majestic moments of divine miracles. I realize that for such learning to happen requires rearranging my priorities to include more time with You. I cannot teach what I do not know. For others truly to see You in me, I must humble myself by being Your student. I must learn before I can lead. Only as my learning translates into action will I be the kind of pupil You want me to be.

With love,
Marsha

A Lesson for the Least of These

Dear Child:

Take a lesson from the ants, you lazy fellow. Learn from their ways and be wise! For though they have no king to make them work, yet they labor hard all summer, gathering food for the winter. But you—all you do is sleep. When will you wake up? "Let me sleep a little longer!" Sure, just a little more! And as you sleep, poverty creeps upon you like a robber and destroys you; want attract you in full armor.

Therefore, take care to follow the commands, decrees and laws I give you today.

Away from me, you evildoers, that I may keep the commands of my God!

Trouble and distress have come upon me, but your commands are my delight.

Yet you are near, O Lord, and all your commands are true.

Keeping God's commands is what counts. Each one should remain in the situation which he was in when God called him.

This is how we know that we love the children of God: by loving God and carrying out his commands. This is love for God: to obey his commands. And his commands are not burdensome, for everyone born of God overcomes the world.

Hold on to instruction, do not let it go; guard it well, for it is your life.

Your Father
(Prov. 6:6-11, TLB; Deut. 7:11; Pss. 119:115,143,151; 1 Cor. 7:19-20; 1 John 5:2-4; Prov. 4:13)

119
A Lesson for the Least of These

Dear Father:

Your letters are clear. They have provided precise commands and instructions for those seeking wisdom. When I choose to follow Your way, I am on my path to the victorious Christian life. Let's face it. Following someone else's instructions is difficult. Yet, I am relieved to find that Your letters provide clear directions. In our relationship I am comforted to know that Someone else is in charge. I know that sounds strange. So often I "choose" to be in charge. But, Father, when I am tired and worn, I need someone else to command my life. I know I need to let You be in charge all of the time, not just when I do not feel up to par. *Being in charge* means being responsible. I want You to be the author and perfecter of my faith—the One ultimately responsible for my growth, development, and total life.

Often I struggle with my will. The thread of will is woven with the thread of conscious choices. In fact, the two are so tightly woven that they may appear the same. This became evident to me last evening.

I was speaking at a women's retreat in the East. After the evening meal, I decided to go on a short nature walk to clear my mind and be alone with You. It was a beautiful summer evening.

In the woods, I noticed something I have seen many times, but I had never been so captivated by it. I watched an army of ants march strategically in line, each carrying something toward a mound of dirt. I suppose they were building their winter home and storing extra food. I remember thinking, *Someone else is in charge here.* I was reminded of what you said in Proverbs 6: "Take a lesson from the ants. . . ."

Yes, someone bigger than me is in charge of the ants. Even Albert Einstein recognized this. He wrote, "A spirit is manifest in the laws of the universe, vastly superior to that of man, and one in the face of which we without modest powers must feel humble. Causality has to exist. The universe could not operate on chance. God does not play dice."

Often, my personal and professional responsibilities seem overwhelming. At times, I feel responsible for everyone, everywhere, every minute! But I feel so relieved when I recognize that I am not in charge of everything. In fact, I am never in charge. I am just responsible to the One who commands and instructs the universe. You are in charge of it all. You merely call me to the cause.

Father, You are in control and have a perfect will for my life. How I

With Love, Marsha

fit and merge into Your will becomes a matter of choice. You have placed me in a position to choose. You do not create human beings to be robots. You create living beings who are free to choose. I have a hard time comprehending what it means to live in Your will. How do I become centered in You? I am convinced that it is not a matter of intellectual discernment. It is a state of heart. It should be implicit to my life and as natural as breathing.

Father, how do I find Your will? I acknowledge it is always there. Discovering it is sometimes difficult. Discovery begins as I renew my mind and heed Your letters, is deepened as I obey them, and continues as I become rightly related to You. Through discovering and applying Your will, I become free to be more like me, which You created.

Saying yes to Your will is saying yes to a disciplined life. Where do Your will and my will merge? If I forget that there are two wills and dwell only on Your sovereign will, I abdicate my responsibility. Yet, if I forget Your sovereignty and see myself as independent, I leave You out of the picture. In both cases, I fail to do Your will; the result is forfeiting my joy and freedom.

Your letters remind me that You have arranged my day in such a way that Your action is to be coupled with my actions. I am nudged about this as I examine the repeated examples of how You chose to use sinful and weak men and women to accomplish Your perfect purpose. You actually allowed these persons the dignity to choose willfully to be a part of what You were doing.

Father, You have given me that same choice today. Such choices are humbling. They demand faith in You. Exercising my faith provides one of the greatest joys of my Christian life. Someone bigger than myself is in charge. What a relief and joy it is when I sincerely merge my life and will with Yours.

With love,
Marsha

Be Thou My Vision

Dear Child:
 Then you will win favor and a good name in the sight of God and man.
 The blind receive sight, the lame walk, those who have leprosy are cured, the deaf hear, the dead are raised, and the good news is preached to the poor.
 We live by faith, not by sight.
 But, everything exposed by the light becomes visible, for it is light that makes everything visible.

Your Father
(Prov. 3:4; Matt. 11:5; 2 Cor. 5:7; Eph. 5:13)

With Love, Marsha

Dear Father:

Of all my senses, I believe my eyes are the most important to me. Without my sight I could not read Your letters (except through Braille, of course). That thought never occurred to me until this moment. How precious is my sight. Thank You, Father, for two healthy eyes.

Four-fifths of all I remember is what I have seen, from the beauty of the sun setting behind the mountains to learning in school. Perhaps even more amazing is my "view pad"—my eye is no larger than a coin or postage stamp. Pictures of Your world are detected by nerve cells inside that tiny area. The eye is miraculous. Each time light strikes an object in my view, it generates a nerve signal which travels from my eye to my brain. My brain receives millions of simultaneous reports from my eyes. My eyes then turn light rays into nerve impulses and send them to my brain. My brain actually does the seeing.

I use my eyes for more than sight. I use them to show my love and concern. I cry. Sometimes my eyes even show my joy and laughter. Strangely enough, for about half an hour each day my eyes cannot see—they are blinking. This one-third-second sweep is Your delicate means of keeping my eyes' surface clean. You thought of everything!

My sight has not always been good. I remember the exact moment when my parents realized my eyesight was failing. I must have been in the fifth grade. Annually each child had the standard big "E" eye exam—lining up and reading the chart. For the first time I could not read the letters. Mrs. Freeman sent a note to Mother and Daddy, indicating they needed to have my eyes checked by a trained professional.

I remember the eye exam. Instead of a poster-like chart on the wall, Dr. Garrett used a huge green machine that projected letters, lines, and colors. He asked: "Is this better or is this better?" With each question, he inserted a glass lens into the machine. After the exam, Dr. Garrett told Mom the news: "Mrs. Spradlin, Marsha has myopia."

I was terrified. *Myopia?* I wondered. *Could I die from it?* Soon, Dr. Garrett noticed my concern. He then focused his attention on the ten-year-old patient and explained that myopia was a rather simple eye defect commonly known as nearsightedness.

"You probably inherited it from your mother," Dr. Garrett observed. "*Myopia* means that you can see things nearby but not far away."

Be Thou My Vision

"Can you fix it?" I asked.

"Fortunately! We'll fix you up with a pair of pretty glasses," explained Dr. Garrett.

Glasses! Neat, I thought. For the next half hour, Mom and I examined the countless frames. I tried on each at least once. I picked blue ones, just like my friend, Debbie, had. I thought the two weeks would never arrive until my glasses would be ready. I could hardly wait to see what I would look like. It had not occurred to me that the world would look different, too.

When I picked up my new glasses, I was stunned as we drove home. For the first time, I realized that each tree had individual leaves. I could read road signs and see things that had been there all along. Without glasses, I had not been able to capture the wondrous details of God's creation or even the printed messages on the signs lining the highway. My new eyesight expanded my world. In many ways, I saw my world for the first time.

Since then, my lenses have been changed dozens of times. They are now very thick in size. Fortunately, contact lenses camouflage my lack of good sight. Yet, without the aid of artificial lenses, my world is still a blur. I can see only within a three-inch range of my eyes. My myopia has worsened. But, with corrective lenses, my sight is still perfect! I totally depend on my lenses for my daily routines and to keep my world view in perspective.

Father, I often wonder if I do not suffer from a spiritual disorder—spiritual myopia. Perhaps I need a spiritual "I" exam. I often see the needs of others near me but fail to see the needs of those who are not directly within view. Fortunately, this can be corrected. Father, give me correct vision. Train my eyes to focus clearly on needs near and far. I may need to have my spiritual lenses adjusted from time to time—maybe daily. I must totally depend on You for added strength in sight.

Father, another eye defect that I do not have physically, but I do suffer from on occasions—spiritually—is *hyperopia*. It is the opposite of nearsightedness. Hyperopia is the inability to see nearby. Yet, sufferers do have the ability to see distances. Sometimes Father, I am sympathetic, caring, and understanding with those outside my private world. I find it much easier to become critical of family members. I am even guilty of ministering to those "across the waters," while I let my neighbor go hungry. Father, please check my spiritual sight. Let me have a compassionate vision for all people, near and far. The time may come that I need spiritual bifocals. I may need Your help in seeing both near and far. I am so grateful that You know my needs and can correct any spiritual visual defect. My responsibility is to approach you and confess the problem. Only then can You restore my sight.

Yes, I rank my eyes as most important. Is this true for everyone? Maybe I give such status to my sight because of my life-style. Sometimes the society I live in clouds my vision. I begin to view the janitor as less important than the pilot. Father, when this happens, remind me to reconsider what I rank as important. For example, are my eyes more important than my hands? Yes, we live in a society in which the janitor has less status and value, because he is "replaceable." But, in the Body's division of labor, is status so important? It may be immaterial to the task I am called to do.

Father, I know I have suffered from this serious spiritual disorder. Often I have become so overwhelmed by the many pressures in my life that I see nothing except what is directly in front of me—straight ahead. And, even then, it is cloudy and out of perspective because I am tired and out of Your control. I have lost my ability to focus clearly on anything. The physical treatment is an eye drop to lubricate the eye's lens. My spiritual eyes and entire life need to be lubricated and bathed in Your Spirit. I need spiritual restoration. That may be the only remedy to restore my spiritual sight.

Father, thank You for two eyes that can see. May my focus be constantly on You. Only then can I look to Your fields and know that they are ready to be harvested. As I look and respond to what I see, I demonstrate what it means to be Yours.

With love,
Marsha

Feed My Sheep

Dear Child:

"Do you truly love me more than these?... Feed my lambs... Do you truly love me?... Take care of my sheep... Do you love me?... Feed my sheep."

The Lord is my shepherd, I shall not be in want. He makes me lie down in green pastures, he leads me beside quiet waters, he restores my soul.

Know that the Lord is God. It is he who made us, and we are his; we are his people, the sheep of his pasture.

The Lord's people will not be like sheep without a shepherd.

Your Father
(John 21:15-17; Pss. 23:1-3; 100:3; Num. 27:17)

With Love, Marsha

Dear Father:

As I rode through the barren terrain of New Mexico, I noticed something scattered about the rugged mountain slopes. They resembled white, puffy dots. Not sure what I was seeing, I asked my friend to stop so I could look more closely. "Those are sheep. Haven't you seen sheep before?" my friend asked. Other than the stuffed-animal type in Christmas pageants, I hadn't. They looked nothing like I expected. I thought they would be lily white—spotless. I was so intrigued that I took several photos of them.

My interest intensified as I recalled what You wrote about sheep, the shepherd, and the pasture. Your language is so graphic. You paint symbolic pictures explaining Your mysteries. Even as I wanted my friend to stop the van so I could have a closer look at the sheep, I wanted to become better acquainted with the meaning of Your letters. I want to become a sheep expert.

I started my research. I reread everything You said about sheep. I learned that you spoke through men of humble origin. Much of the terminology and teaching is couched in rural language. Much of your communication deals with outdoor subjects and natural phenomenon—familiar to the nomadic folk of long ago. You used nature to explain supernatural truths. As a twentieth-century urban woman, I was not well acquainted with livestock, crops, land, and wildlife. Without this background, I had missed some of Your truth.

"Feed my sheep." These must be pivotal words. Lord, You repeated that phrase to Peter. After doing my homework, I realized that You packed each word with powerful meaning that I can apply today.

Feed.—*Freedom from fear.*—Before sheep can be fed, basic sheep needs must be met. One of these is freedom. They are timid by nature. They must feel comfort and security. A frightened sheep will not eat.

Freedom from friction.—Strangely enough, sheep experience social friction. If there is friction within the flock, none of the sheep will eat.

Freedom from parasites.—If something is a burden or "eating at them," sheep will not eat.

Freedom from hunger.—If sheep are hungry, they will not follow the shepherd, even if he is leading them to food.

My.—This word shows possession. The shepherd did not necessarily

Feed My Sheep

own the sheep, but he loved them as if they were his own. And he probably had a close relationship with the owner of the sheep. To love the sheep truly, the good shepherd had to know the sheep, even by name. He had to know their basic needs. Yet, the owner of the sheep had authority over the shepherd. He was ultimately responsible.

Sheep.—Sheep, I have discovered, are basically scared and also not very smart. But their stupidity is often interpreted as innocence. They will follow the shepherd anywhere, but they will only follow the shepherd they know. They will not follow a stranger. They totally depend on the shepherd to keep them away from trouble, rescue them from danger, and lead them to fresh water and green pastures. Green pastures were not plentiful in the psalmist's (nor Jesus' day). In many instances, they are not today, either.

When sheep are thirsty, they became restless and search for water; they drink anything in sight. They did not have the sense not to drink polluted water which would give them diseases or parasites. They depended on the shepherd to lead them to pure water. He often tasted the water himself before allowing them to drink.

Sheep are creatures of habit. They will follow the same trails until they wear ruts into them and graze the same hillsides until they turn into desert. Left to their own, they can be self-destructive without knowing it.

I see application of the phrase "Feed my sheep." Before I can be fed, my basic human needs must be met. I must experience freedom—freedom from fear. Father, I, too, am fearful at times. I am afraid of lacking love and acceptance. And I, on occasion, feel the pangs of intimidation. You have said, "There is no fear in love. But perfect love drives out fear, because fear has to do with punishment. The one who fears is not made perfect in love" (1 John 4:18). Teach me to be free from fear.

Second, in order for You to feed me, I must be free from social friction, even within my Christian community. I must be confident that I can always go to You for rest. Your pasture is a place to rest and retreat from the tensions of tyrannizing urgency that infiltrate my day.

Third, I must feel freedom from parasites and pests. That sounds a little strange. A parasite sucks all the energy and life from the human body. Father, are there parasites draining my spiritual energy? Help me identify them. Do I depend on others for spiritual food? If so, I am the parasite. Or, am I so busy feeding others that I do not find the time to be fed?

Fourth, I must experience freedom from hunger. But what kind of hunger, Father? I remember seeing a woman so depressed that she refused to eat. She was starving. When asked why she would not eat, she remarked, "You don't have anything I want."

My shows a relationship with You, the Good Shepherd. You are also the Authority. You created all Your sheep. You choose who feeds them. As Christians, we are to feed, but we also must take time to be fed. You are the Owner. You choose whom we feed. And You assume the ultimate responsibility. We are to love the flock as our own. Yet, if the sheep do not respond, we are not responsible. As a shepherd, my responsibility is to feed. I cannot eat for them. Likewise, no one can eat for me.

Like sheep, I am basically timid. And like most people, I can follow. Father, help me to be willing to follow You anywhere. Help me not to follow strangers. May my focus be on You, the good and perfect Shepherd.

Teach me to depend on You. Rescue me from trouble and lead me to fresh water and green pastures where my soul can be restored. May I never become so thirsty that I drink anything offered to me. Test the water first, Father. Teach me to drink from Your pure and living water. May it become a daily habit as I spend time with You.

Father, may I not become a creature of habit, so locked into the same trails and daily routines that I turn my green pasture into a desert. This may mean changing pastures from time to time. May I not be afraid to make changes as I follow You. My refusal to follow may result in my own gradual detriment. Just as the sheep is useful by providing wool and meat, may I be useful. Just as the sheep is meek and gentle, may my life be like the meek and gentle nature of the good and perfect Shepherd. And, just as the sheep may be considered stupid at times, let my stupidity be translated into an innocent spirit that depends on You.

With love,
Marsha

Sh'h, Be Still

Dear Child:
Here is my message for you today from my Word:
   Be still, and know that I am God.
   There is a time for everything, and a season for every activity under heaven, . . . a time to be silent and a time to speak.
   Let all the earth be silent before Him.

Your Father
(Ps.46:10; Eccl. 3:1,7; Hab. 2:20*b*)

With Love, Marsha

Dear Father:

Why is it so hard to be silent? Am I such a stranger to myself that I feel discomfort when forced to be alone? Like so many times before, spiritual insights and spiritual sensitivity have come to me wrapped in pain or in "plain" experiences. I felt another plain experience coming this morning when I realized I would be forced to be silent today.

I arose early to prepare for the day. When the phone rang, I realized my inability to speak. My anxiety intensified as I sensed frustration from my friend trying to understand. "I have laryngitis," I whispered.

Throughout the day, I received many good suggestions regarding remedies. The one I found most difficult to put into action was from the expert—my doctor. "Marsha, don't talk!" he suggested.

Easier said than done is a trite but appropriate expression of my experience. My angst increased when I realized that not only was I to remain silent, but I would have to live in solitude for the next three days. *I'll go nuts! I don't know how to be still*, I thought in panic.

But today has been one of the most meaningful days of my life. However, it didn't start that way. At first, I was bothered by silence. I was uncomfortable with the time alone. But this break from the routines and relationships called me from my outer world to meet You in my inner sanctuary of solitude.

I realized today how my world is filled with noise. I have become so accustomed to noise that I have grown restless without it. I have a stereo or radio in almost every room of my house, in my car, and in my office. When I call a friend, I am offered music over the phone, until she comes to answer my call. Endless music, chatter, and the noise of tension fill my "living" room. With the intrusion of so much noise, I have not been able to withdraw and monitor Your still small voice.

I must learn to soundproof my heart against the intruding noise of the outside world in order to hear what You have to say to me, Father. I must not appreciate the terrible conspiracy of noise that has denied me the silence and solitude I need to cultivate my relationship with You. I love the words of Mother Teresa of Calcutta:

> We need to find God, and he cannot be found in noise and restlessness. God is the friend of silence. See how nature—trees, flowers, grass—grow in silence; see the stars, the moon and sun, how they move in si-

131
Sh'h, Be Still

lence... the more we receive in silent prayer, the more we can give in our active life. We need silence to be able to touch souls. The essential thing is not what we say, but what God says to us and through us. All our words will be useless unless they come from within—words which do not give the light of Christ increase the darkness.[1]

Today's experience of silence and solitude did not come easily. At first I equated it with laziness, unproductivity, and inaction. At first my mind was exploding with a list of "must do's." It seemed that the slightest noise outside my tiny bedroom was an intrusion into my concentration toward being still and knowing You.

For a full day I have been alone. One would think that such separation from others would cause me not to feel as close, yet I now feel nearer to them. It is neither physical solitude that separates me from others nor physical isolation... but spiritual isolation. This is true. When I am a stranger to myself, I am estranged from others. Therefore, if I am out of touch with myself, then I cannot touch others.

Thank You, Father, for this day of silence and solitude. During these hours alone with You, I have been in a situation mainly to listen. I have been in the position to rest and rely on You.

Lead me to make regular appointments with You to exercise silence and solitude. During such moments, You have filled my cup. I can now go out and touch the lives of those persons filling the busy hours of my days. May I continue to learn how to listen amid the noise. Teach me to listen with my heart to needs of those around me. Continue to develop within me the ability to communicate Your love in uniquely and creatively. When I am well and strong, teach me to rest and rely on You to equip me, speak through me, and live through my total being.

With love,
Marsha

Note

1. Malcolm Muggeridge, *Something Beautiful for God* (Garden City, N.Y.: Image, 1977), 48.

PART 4:
Your Mercies

"The Lord your God is a merciful God" (Deut. 4:31).

Out of Darkness

Dear Child:

No one lights a lamp and hides it in a jar or puts it under a bed. Instead, he puts it on a stand, so that those who come in can see the light.

You are the light of the world. A city on a hill cannot be hidden. Neither do people light a lamp and put it under a bowl. Instead they put it on its stand, and it gives light to everyone in the house. In the same way, let your light shine before men, that they may see your good deeds and praise your Father in heaven.

The eye is the lamp of the body. If your eyes are good, your whole body will be full of light. But if your eyes are bad, your whole body will be full of darkness. If then the light within you is darkness, how great is that darkness!

In him was life, and that life was the light of men. The light shines in the darkness, but the darkness has not understood it.

I am the light of the world. Whoever follows me will never walk in darkness, but will have the light of life. I have made you a light for the Gentiles, that you may bring salvation to the ends of the earth.

There will be no more night. They will not need the light of a lamp or the light of the sun, for the Lord God will give them light. And they will reign for ever and ever.

Your Father
(Luke 8:16; Matt. 5:14-16; 6:22-23; John 1:4-5; 8:12; Acts 13:47; Rev. 22:5)

With Love, Marsha

Dear Father:

Your letters speak so radiantly about light. I want to understand their full meaning. You helped illumine my understanding on the subject last week on a trip.

I roomed with a friend who was out of sorts one morning while putting on her makeup. With two of us sharing a bathroom, Marti decided to let me have the big mirror. She used her little mirror and "put on her face" by the tiny lamp near her bed.

Aggravated by darkness, she remarked, "A three-way lamp and a one-way bulb." That reminded me of our possibilities as Christians. The three-way lamp was designed to give three levels of brightness. Because the light bulb in its socket was capable of only one level, Marti was able to have only limited light. The lamp was unable to produce the full extent of its power.

Father, You have gifted us with tremendous potential. We have the potential to be that three-way lamp. But we often use only a portion of what You have given us.

My light may be hidden or easily diminished because I do not recognize what resides in me spiritually. Sometimes I do not even use the potential I have already recognized. I make excuses: "I just can't do that as well as she can. I'm just too shy. I'm not as educated, talented, or as attractive. That's just not me. I don't have time. No one appreciates what I do anyway." Each negative thought represents that one-way bulb preventing me from shining and being my brightest for You.

Father, You have bountiful opportunities before me, if I am willing to investigate them in Your light. Only when I am willing to step out, however, will I experience Your power. My most-celebrated blessings have come when I have been myself—the self You designed me to be.

I must admit, I want results. Without results, I feel despair. I may deny my potential, pretend it is not there, but that does not change the fact that as a Christian I want results in winning my world to You.

I do want to reach my potential, Father. Yet, can that actually happen? I am not sure I have ever met a Christian who has reached his or her full potential. It helps to consider Paul's Letter to the Philippians. "Brothers, I do not consider myself yet to have taken hold of it" (Phil. 3:13).

I must be careful, Father. I do not want to become so self-conscious

Out of Darkness

that I will never "take hold of it," become immobilized, and give up. I must continue moving toward the goal You have set for me. Feelings of giving up are destructive and result in self-hate. They focus on myself rather than others. I must learn to relax and enjoy the thrill of the journey of "taking hold of it." Only then will I realize my potential as a witness.

I cannot act positively and realize results only by reading Your letters, going to seminars, and listening to tapes. Those can lead me to action, but they are not the action. The more Spirit-guided action, the more results I will see. The more results I see, the more I realize who I am and whose I am in You.

Father, You have already equipped me with all I need. As I accept my potential, I am in the process of becoming all that You have designed for me to become.

Father, in faith we have arrived. You have planted the seeds of potential within our lives. I must activate the light that is already within. Turning the switch is my choice. Through that act, may others see "Jesus revealed in me."

With love,
Marsha

Come . . . Follow Me

Dear Child:

"Come, follow me," Jesus called, "and I will make you fishers of men."

If anyone would come after me, he must deny himself and take up his cross and follow me. For whoever wants to save his life will lose it, but whoever loses his life for me will find it. What good will it be for a man if he gains the whole world, yet forfeits his soul?

I am the light of the world. Whoever follows me will never walk in darkness, but will have the light of life.

He goes on ahead of them, and his sheep follow him because they know his voice. But they will never follow a stranger; in fact, they will run away from him because they do not recognize a stranger's voice.

Whoever serves me must follow me; and where I am, my servant also will be.

Follow the way of love and eagerly desire spiritual gifts.

To this you were called, because Christ suffered for you, leaving you an example, that you should follow in his steps.

Your Father
(Matt. 4:19; 16:21; John 8:12; 10:4-5; 12:26; 1 Cor. 14:1; 1 Pet. 2:21)

Come... Follow Me

Dear Father:

Your letters continue to mesh with the patterns of the ordinary strains of my plain-vanilla life. Each one, when applied to my daily experiences, gives strength to the countless threads woven into variegated patterns. The patterns make my plain-vanilla life extraordinary.

After reading Your letter today, I tried to summarize Your teachings about what it means to follow You. The teachings are so simple that most people stumble over them. Your teachings at this point remind me of the little rule I learned as a child before crossing a railroad track: "Stop, look, and listen."

To be a follower, I must stop where I am going long enough to find You and learn Your directions. I must look. Otherwise, I could follow the wrong leader. Looking toward You means a clarity of direction—not confusion. Looking not only gives direction for the course of my life but in some cases a destination. Your letters become my road maps as I venture out on my journey. Yet, often, regardless how hard I try, I am not sure of the destination—only the journey. That is where listening fits. I must listen to Your directions. I must hear only Your voice. That means quieting my own spirit, wishes, and desires. It means listening to no other leader. Only as I listen will I stay on course. Yet, another step was not included in my basic railroad-crossing training. *Follow!* I can stop, look, and listen, and still not follow. To follow is my choice—a deliberate action.

Father, it is so easy to stray from the course. Only last week, You taught me a lesson about following the wrong leader. After a busy day at the office, several friends and I decided to eat dinner together and celebrate the completion of another day. Chinese food! Since I had not been to the restaurant before, I decided to follow my friend Mickey. Her shiny new car was creamy lavender and sleek. I had seen it, but I had not seen her drive it until we left the office.

Once on the interstate, I did something that's common for me. I shifted my brain into neutral—"autopilot" I call it. After several miles of neutral driving, I realized I was supposed to be going somewhere. Where was Mickey? I quickly shifted out of autopilot as I began to scan the interstate for Mickey. My eyes searched for her *old car,* which was red. I found one and was not sure how she had gone so far ahead.

I pulled carefully into the left lane in a noble attempt to catch up with

With Love, Marsha

that red car. I managed to merge and maneuver in and out of traffic until I was close behind. Exactly in time! Mickey's red car was signaling to turn at the next exit. I followed.

We meandered up and down unfamiliar roads. I was feeling safe. Mickey certainly knew where we were going. After several minutes of traveling the unfamiliar roads, I remembered one friend mentioning that the restaurant was not more than ten minutes from the office. I glanced at my watch. Twenty minutes had passed. Pangs of insecurity began to sweep over me. I felt I had no choice but to follow. Even if I decided to follow, I was stuck. I had followed Mickey so far off the interstate that I was lost. While following, I discovered parts of the city that I had never seen before. Soon, we pulled into a nice neighborhood. *This is a strange place for a restaurant*, I thought. The next turn was into the driveway of an attractive two-story house. I followed. The *gentleman* inside the red car stepped out and looked at me. He was not Mickey. Too embarrassed to tell the stranger what I had done, I merely waved as I backed out of the driveway.

I drove several moments lost in unfamiliar territory. My confusion was compounded, knowing my friends would be concerned about me. More than half an hour had passed since we left the office.

I could ask for help, I thought. That was out. Who could help someone who did not know where she was going? I had not bothered to ask the name of the restaurant.

"Stop, look, listen." Those words came to mind. I asked myself, *Where are you going?* The only place I could go was home. It was familiar. It meant safety. I proceeded to look for clues. How could I get home without knowing where I was? I listened. I could hear the cars on the interstate. I knew if I could reach the interstate, I could find my way back home. I did! Home never felt as safe.

I flung open the door and dropped my briefcase as I reached for the phone book. My eyes scanned the pages of Chinese restaurants. *I think I will recognize it if I see it*, I thought. *There it is, I think.* Pacing through the living room with the phone in one hand, I dialed the number and asked for Mickey. I was lucky. It was the right restaurant, and the receptionist found Mickey. I explained the best I could. I could tell by the sound of her voice that Mickey had been concerned, and I sensed her relief. I also overheard gales of laughter coming from the table of my

Come . . . Follow Me

friends hearing the story secondhand. It was too late to join them. I enjoyed a quiet evening at home thinking about "stop, look, and listen."

Stop! Father, teach me to stop before I venture out. May I not become so busy that I neglect my own responsibility to receive specific instructions from You. May I never shift my spiritual life into autopilot, but constantly keep my focus on You as my leader.

Look! May I look to You for leadership. May I question the directions from time to time, only to reaffirm that You are the one leading me. May I be on the lookout for false leaders—drivers of spurious red cars!

Listen! May I listen without fail. I listen as I scan the pages of Your letters for familiar words and new directions from You. I listen as I pray and as I seek Your face.

Follow! I can stop, look, and listen and still be confused until my following is an active response to Your voice. In times, I follow by faith. I do not always know where You are leading me. But, I know that You will be careful to give me each piece of information at the moment it is needed.

With love,
Marsha

A Course in Humility

Dear Child:
 God opposes the proud but gives grace to the humble.
 Humble yourselves before the Lord, and he will lift you up.
 He guides the humble in what is right and teaches them his ways.

Your Father
(Jas. 4:6,10; Ps. 25:9)

A Course in Humility

Dear Father:

Yesterday I had a cram course in humility. Impatiently, I worked my way through the crowd to the baggage-claim area at the airport. As a seemingly infinite collection of bags passed by on the conveyor belt, my impatience grew. *Certainly my bag has not been lost*, I thought. Lost baggage is the ultimate dread of a seasoned traveler. That nauseous emotion intensified as I remembered that for the first time I had checked *everything*—speeches for the seminar I was to lead, not to mention personal essentials like toothbrush and makeup. *Be calm*, I thought. *It must be somewhere*. I was almost ashamed to know that You were watching.

Slowly each piece was claimed, except a brown garment bag. My luggage was blue! The crowd had disappeared. *It's time to panic!* I cried within. I had made it to Kansas, but my belongings had not. The autumn wind makes it cold in Kansas. My coat was in the suitcase!

I walked to the baggage-claim office to fill out a missing-luggage report. As I filed my claim, I wondered how I would teach without my outlines. *Without makeup, how could I possibly stand in front of seminar participants? Maybe I should catch the next plane back home.*

I didn't fly back home. Instead, I completed my assignment. It was a classic opportunity to learn the true meaning of humility. I learned a lesson in receiving, recognizing limitations, relying on others as a source of support, and depending on You to be seen and heard through me.

As I prepared to speak, I wondered, *Could these people go beyond my limitation to see Your abundant strength? Could my weakness become Your strength? Could my humility be Your magnificence?*

You taught me so much during these twenty-four hours. I learned it is OK to wear the same outfit two days in a row; I can shampoo my hair with bar soap; seminar participants enjoy sharing makeup and other essentials; and when I am weakest and speechless, Your voice is strong and overflowing. I learned that my concerns were already taken care of.

Your letters had already answered my questions. What should I wear? First Peter 5:5 explained: "Be clothed with humility" (KJV). What will I say? Proverbs 11:2 assured me that with humility comes wisdom. But the real question was not what I would wear or what I would say, but why I had to wait until I was in a bind to learn Your

With Love, Marsha

great truths about humility. Father, can I experience the fullness that accompanies humility when I am not in a desperate situation?

Thank You for Your letter. Your Word was right on the line. I am convinced that humility must be a state of being, an attitude, a life-style. Humility does not have to be coupled with desperation but determination to let You control my every thought, action, and motive.

How humble am I? How often do I walk, speak, and lead in Your strength? How concerned am I with what I have defined as essential only to neglect to recognize that You have already cared for my needs?

How can I redirect my interest from what I have toward who You are? I am challenged to develop a desperate heart for Your likeness and likemindedness. As I do, perhaps I will encourage others to live in truth, humility, and righteousness (Ps. 45:5).

With love,
Marsha

Make Up Your Mind

Dear Child:
Here is my message for you today from my Word:
  Love the Lord your God with all your heart and with your soul and with all your mind.
  All the believers were one in heart and mind.
  Do not conform any longer to the pattern of this world, but be transformed by the renewing of your mind. Then you will be able to test and approve what God's will is—his good, pleasing and perfect will.
  To be made new in the attitude of your minds, and to put on the new self, created to be like God in true righteousness and holiness.
  Set your minds on things above, not on earthly things.
  "For who has known the mind of the Lord that he may instruct him?" But we have the mind of Christ.
  For God did not give us a spirit of timidity, but a spirit of power, of love, and of self-discipline.

Your Father
(Matt. 22:37; Acts 4:32; Rom. 12:2; Eph. 4:23-24; Col. 3:1; 1 Cor. 2:16; 2 Tim. 1:7)

With Love, Marsha

Dear Father:

Standing in line gave me plenty of time to think about what I was doing. Fear and doubt crept in. *I am over thirty-five years old. What am I doing here?* repeatedly darted in and out of my mind. As I gazed across the rows of individuals in each line, I realized I was one of the oldest. Yet, I felt excited—like a schoolgirl again.

Going back to college at my age was no easy decision. I felt Your leadership urging me to return to school for post-graduate studies. But our minds quickly become shifted to neutral once we graduate. I questioned if I would be able to keep up. After all, I had a full-time, responsible job that already required more hours than I had in a day. Squeezing in additional study time seemed ridiculous.

After I registered, I spent the afternoon in the university book store. I cannot believe I was so excited about buying notebooks, textbooks, and pencils. Why wasn't I that enthusiastic in my previous college days?

That semester proved several truths to me. I can squeeze in one more project, if I first determine it is valuable. Sure, it required a few days to retrain myself to listen, take notes, study during lunch break at work, and concentrate. Yet, the amount of information my mind could absorb seemed considerable. You have given people minds capable of incredible growth and maturity.

As I read Your letters, I realize how much You emphasize the mind. You refer to the word *mind* roughly 200 times. If I understand the original Hebrew and Greek correctly, the English word *mind* does not do justice to what You mean. For example, sometimes Your word *mind* means soul, heart, and attitude.

I am astounded when I consider all I have learned in my lifetime, the past ten years, the past month, yesterday! No, I do not stop learning once I stop growing physically, unless I choose to.

How does the magnificent mind work, Father? My mind is more than a computer. Modern neurological research has given me a new appreciation for the strategic role of my mind. Inside my brain are about 100 billion living cells called neurons. Each can interact in multiple ways with every other neuron. The number of interconnections within my brain is estimated to be in the order of 10 to the 800th power! Father, that time is more than the number of atoms in the entire universe!

I do not understand how it works, Father, but the human brain is

Make Up Your Mind

truly one of Your most miraculous creations. I know it receives information—sensation. I learn through seeing and hearing, as well as internal sensation.

I know my mind interprets. You did not create a mind that is preprogrammed. Instead, You gave me a mind that can think, make decisions, and grow. I realize that much of my thinking is influenced by past or present experiences or my environment. My mind is also capable of influencing my behavior. That happens as I talk to myself. What I say to myself usually determines how I act. Perhaps that is why Your letters insist that we think good thoughts. Thinking good must come before being good. You have promised me perfect peace, if I focus and place my trust in You: "Finally, brothers, whatever is true, whatever is noble, whatever is right, whatever is pure, whatever is lovely, whatever is admirable—if anything is excellent or praiseworthy—think about such things" (Phil. 4:8).

You have instructed me to develop the mind of Christ. Father, teach me to do that. What do I really know about Jesus' mind, anyway? You have shown me in Your letters that Jesus knew the Scriptures, was constantly aware of You, and sensitive to the guidance of the Holy Spirit.

Jesus had a caring mind. In teaching the disciples, He stated that the greatest characteristic of a Christian must be love. He also had an informed mind. His mind was clear and alert to danger. He was able to make plans and capable of coping with the stresses of life. Jesus had a heavenly mind. The Christian mind is set on things above, not on earthly things. He also had an obedient mind. Often, He mentioned His desire to submit to Your will.

Father, teach me to think about how my mind can become like His. I realize I cannot develop the mind of Christ by studying and trying harder. Only the Holy Spirit alone can empower me to live in the joy You have planned for me.

With love,
Marsha

Teachable Moment

Dear Child:

Train a child in the way he should go, and when he is old he will not turn from it.

Train yourself to be godly. For physical training is of some value, but godliness has value for all things, holding promise for both the present life and the life to come.

A student is not above his teacher, but everyone who is fully trained will be like his teacher.

Do not exasperate your children; instead, bring them up in the training and instruction of the Lord.

Everyone who competes in the games goes into strict training. They do it to get a crown that will not last; but we do it to get a crown that will last forever.

All Scripture is God-breathed and is useful for teaching, rebuking, correcting and training in righteousness, so that the man of God may be thoroughly equipped for every good work.

Your Father
(Prov. 22:6; 1 Tim. 4:7-8; Luke 6:40; Eph. 6:4; 1 Cor. 9:25; 2 Tim. 3:16-17)

Teachable Moment

Dear Father:

Throughout my life, significant people have crossed my path. Some have made vivid impressions that will live with me forever. Your letter reminded me of one person from my childhood whose imprint can be seen in every word I write. She was a teacher, trainer, and friend.

I was frightened the day I saw my name posted underneath hers. I was one of thirty students listed for her fourth-grade class. The third-grade hall talk had provided enough information to inject terrifying anticipation into summer vacation. Which unlucky ones would be the young cadets enlisted in her little army? She was known to be the hardest fourth-grade teacher at Whistler Elementary School. She was the plague and scourge of many nine-year-old children. She ran her class with the authority of a military sergeant.

I'll never pass! was my immediate thought when I realized I would be her student. The only consoling thought was that Peggy and Pam, my closest friends from the three previous grades, were also among the unfortunate—the *Les Miserables*.

Maybe Mother can talk Mr. Kelly into moving me to Mrs. Jefferson's room, I desperately conjectured.

After the third day of classes, I was surprised I had survived. I did not want to like her, but I did. The rumors were true. She was the hardest teacher I had ever had, but some quality of hers motivated me. I was pleasantly surprised to discover that, rather than being a harsh, military-type leader, she was caring and very attractive.

For the first month of school, I sat quietly in my assigned seat and spoke not a word. I was still scared of her. Why? I had never heard her raise her voice, even though we all knew when we were being reprimanded for misbehaving.

In November there was a wonderful occurrence. Actually, it was a bad happening that later entered the realm of the wonderful. After school one day, I had a bicycle accident. The result was several scratches and abrasions and a broken arm. Daddy rushed home from work and rushed me to Dr. Hamilton's office across the street from school.

I can still smell the aroma of the doctor's office and remember sitting on the edge of the examining table, my feet dangling to one side, waiting

With Love, Marsha

for the doctor to announce the results of the X-rays. Daddy sat patiently with me. His presence was so comforting.

The doctor stuck his head into the waiting room and announced, "It's broken for a fact, but we'll fix that. Young lady, we are going to put a pretty little cast on that arm. In about a month, it will be as good as new. But no more bicycle acrobatics!" the doctor half scolded.

The cast weighed almost as much as I. It felt awkward at first. I remember the special attention from Mother that evening. She cooked my favorite dessert and nursed my broken spirit. After I was in bed, I overheard her telephone conversation with my teacher.

Early the next morning, as Mother helped me dress, she said, "I talked to Miss Ivey last night. She said you don't have to stand outside in line holding your books while you wait for the bell to ring. As long as you have the cast, she wants you to come inside before the bell rings."

What will I say to her? I asked myself. I had hardly spoken a word in class. I was mortified to spend time alone with her in the classroom.

Twenty minutes before the bell's familiar ring, Miss Ivey unlocked the door and gazed over the heads of her little troop lined up to greet her. "Marsha, come on inside," she invited as she motioned with her hand.

My fears were relieved when I realized I did not have to talk. She did. During the month, Miss Ivey gave me special jobs to do while we waited for class to begin. I watered the plants, fed the fish, put names on the "today's jobs" board, and watched her carefully straighten each desk, checking for exact uniformity.

After the doctor removed my cast, Miss Ivey did not halt the special attention. The bond grew. I needed extra training to regain my skills in writing.

Each morning, Miss Ivey unlocked the door and gave her familiar signal for me to enter. For twenty minutes, she lovingly retrained the weak motor muscles in my hand. Perhaps the extra attention motivated me to want to retain all the words she spoke. Yet, I now remember nothing she said during those weeks. What I recall are her loving actions. Each morning, she wrote two or three sentences on the green chalkboard. I simply copied them. But, before writing on the board, she sat next to me and let me watch her write each word. I watched her every move. I tried to copy her exactly.

151
Teachable Moment

Miss Ivey had beautiful handwriting in spite of the fact that she gripped the pencil with a straight thumb. Wanting to do exactly as she did, I began to grip my pencil with a straight thumb. I concentrated almost as much on keeping my thumb straight as writing the words with correct style and precision.

The months of extra training formed a bond between student and teacher that did not end at the end of the school year. Over twenty years have passed. Throughout the years, we have maintained close contact. She is still my teacher, but as I grew into adulthood, she became my friend.

During a lunch visit one Christmas, I recalled the writing episode. I showed her how I still wrote with a straight thumb. I then asked how she learned to write with such an interesting grip. She laughed in disbelief. "I broke my thumb in the fourth grade. It healed stiff."

Each time I write, I think about the influence significant individuals have had on my life. Father, what kind of influence do I have on the lives of others? I have realized that those I train will remember what I do more than what I say. Give me insight and wisdom to be the model and example that follows Your life-style.

With love,
Marsha

What's Your Excuse?

Dear Child:

No one whose hope is in you will ever be put to shame, but they will be put to shame who are treacherous without excuse.

For since the creation of the world God's invisible qualities—his eternal power and divine nature—have been clearly seen, being understood from what has been made, so that men are without excuse.

You, therefore, have no excuse, you who pass judgment on someone else, for at whatever point you judge the other, you are condemning yourself, because you who pass judgment do the same things.

Your Father
(Ps.25:3, Rom. 1:20; 2:1)

What's Your Excuse?

Dear Father:

As I write this, the Christmas season is over. The focus of people in our society tends to frustrate me. Instead of celebrating You, we disguise the celebration in commercial commotion.

I found the rush back to the shopping mall to exchange unwanted items worse than the race to pursue the perfect gift. I couldn't help being amused as I stood in the exchange line. Maybe we should call it the *excuse* line.

"Number twenty-nine, what's your excuse?" the cashier asked.

"What's my excuse?" the shopper asked back.

"Are you number twenty-nine?" the cashier inquired again.

"Yes!" the shopper replied.

"Well, is it too long? Too small? Too dark? Too light? Wrong size? Wrong color? Doesn't work? You already have one? Too traditional looking? What's your reason for returning this gift?" she inquired.

"Oh! Now I understand," came back the impatient shopper as she pulled the garment out of the barely opened gift box still bound with ribbon. "It's simply not me."

"Do you have your receipt?" questioned the cashier.

"Oh, no! I've already told you it was a gift," the shopper explained.

"In that case, I cannot give you a cash refund, but you may make another selection. Feel free to find something more fitting—something that is *you!*" the cashier instructed.

Yes, Father, this conversation did amuse me. I wondered if it could have been avoided if the giver had spent more effort and attention selecting the gift. But perhaps the excuse were legitimate. After all, it is hard to choose gifts for some individuals. Some folks seem to have everything. Others we do not know well enough to make an intelligent selection. Smart gift shopping comes down to two points: how well you know the recipient and how aware you are of the available choices.

What made this conversation funny was its similarity to conversations Christians have about so many aspects of their spiritual lives. For example:

"Have you found a church yet?" the woman asked.

"Not yet," the man answered.

"Why not? There are so many great churches in the area," she pointed out.

"I know. I have tried them all, but so far, I haven't found one that's really me," he explained.

"Not you?" she asked.

"Yeah! One church was too small. I thought I would get claustrophobia! Another was too large—I lost my car in the parking lot. One was sort of stuffy; another didn't seem involved enough in the work of the denomination; one was too traditional; and then there was one that was so far out!" he went on.

"Are you saying in this city—with so many choices—and you can't find a church that fits?" she implored.

Sound familiar? Perhaps you have either had such a conversation or overheard one, as I did in the break room at work. Walking back to my office, I pondered my new friend's consternation about finding a "church that fit." I wondered about the number of hours we spend trying to find the *perfect church*. You know, the one with everything custom designed to meet our every need and at the same time meet every whim and fancy of every member. Then, I imagined the dismay my friend would feel when she found that church only to discover later it was not a perfect fit.

I wonder if we could avoid this indecision by directing more effort and attention toward selecting a church. Maybe finding a church *is* like selecting a special gift for a friend. Our choices should hinge on how well we know ourselves and how well we know the choices.

Yet, somehow "church shopping" is different. After all, the church is a gift to us. How much time and energy do we spend dwelling on reasons why a church doesn't fit rather than spending time and energy on the results? Perhaps there are two kinds of people who receive the gift of the church—those with reasons and those with results.

Father, a good giver goes beyond the obvious in making a selection. He or she also considers the reasons. What is the reason for the church? Is it for the gratification of its members? Of course not. The church has a mission. I have always felt that missions is one part of the church's work in fulfilling its total purpose.

Father, isn't missions what the church does in keeping with Your Great Commission as sovereign Lord? Doesn't it extend Your witness and ministry beyond our community of faith to point all persons to Christ and thereby glorify You?

155
What's Your Excuse?

Teach me, Father, how I really fit into my church. Help me realize that I am a vital part in helping my church recognize its responsibility to promote and support the total missions effort.

I can spend all of my time and energy wondering if I fit. Or, I can spend it promoting and supporting the missions enterprise of my church.

Father, I believe there is a church for everyone—a perfect fit. But the only way many of us realize if it fits is to try it on.

With love,
Marsha

Falling Forward

Dear Child:

The Lord delights in a man's way, e he makes his steps steps firm; though he stumble, he will not fall, for the Lord upholds him with his hand.

Cast your cares on the Lord and he will sustain you; he will never let the righteous fall.

The Lord upholds all those who fall and lifts up all who are bowed down.

Whoever trust in his riches will fall, but the righteous will thrive like a green leaf.

Your Father
(Pss. 37:23-24; 55:22; 145:14; Prov. 11:28)

Falling Forward

Dear Father:

Tasting defeat is clearly bittersweet. The defeat is bitter, yet it can result in sweet growth. But tasting the same defeat and making the same mistake repeatedly is humiliation. Humiliation is especially difficult when you go into a challenge confident you will win. That was my feeling as a once-in-a-lifetime experience turned into a flop.

Growing up in South Alabama almost meant spending winter barefoot. I remember Christmas commercials showing fireplaces and snow. I felt deprived. Watching the winter Olympics was inspiring. Snow skiing and figure skating on the glass-like arena of ice seemed incredible. *When I grow up, I am going to be a skier,"* I dreamed.

I consider mid-thirties grown up. The opportunity to learn to snow ski did not come a year too soon. If I waited much longer, I would be unable even to walk around in skis, much less conquer the white mountain slopes.

Early Saturday morning, I flew to Amarillo, Texas, to meet Karen, Jim, and their two children. Each was a veteran skier. I was confident that all I had to do to become expert myself was merely to keep my balance. But to make sure I was prepared, I went to the library to read up on the sport. I also began increasing the distance I jogged to get in better physical shape. Too, I prepared several small snack kits to tuck into my ski jacket for extra energy, while I soared down the slopes with the greatest of ease. I had peanuts and raisins—quick protein and carbohydrates—the perfect choice for the health-minded skier.

Karen stood inside the airport terminal in layers of clothes. "Over here, Marsh!" (many of my friends drop the final *a*) she waved in greeting. "Wait until you see the snow. We had a blizzard last night. Instead of waiting until morning to drive to Red River, Jim and the kids are loaded in the van. We think we should leave tonight. Otherwise, we may not get in."

"Sounds great to me," I exulted.

We gathered my baggage and survival kits and met Jim and the children, waiting in the van. The snow was incredible. It was knee-deep in Amarillo. I couldn't imagine what it must be like in New Mexico.

I sat in the middle seat with one child on each side. After hugs and greetings, we started our late-night drive 200 miles northwest. Mugs of coffee and hot chocolate were welcomed commodities. As we traveled

With Love, Marsha

and sipped, Alan and Joni, ten and eight years old, began to explain how to ski. I felt a little intimidated. These kids were one third my age. What could they possibly teach me? I had read the best books to be found. I had practiced in the privacy of my bedroom. I was fully prepared physically, emotionally, and mentally. I had even visualized myself gracefully skiing down the mountain and overhearing people comment on my style, form, and agility. To be courteous, I listened to my young travel companions.

We arrived in time to find a lodge, unpack the van, and grab about three hours of sleep. The sun had not risen when Karen entered my room with orange juice and hot orange Danishes. "Eat it all, Marsh! You'll need it," she laughed as she shut my door.

Within an hour we were fed, dressed, and in the van. Jim stopped at a local ski-rental shop to pick up my equipment. It had not occurred to me that I needed to rent skis. Not only did I need skis, but also poles, gloves, goggles, and about $50 worth of additional gear. "It's worth it," I justified. "After all, this is a lifetime dream come true."

Getting fitted for the skis and poles was an education. I had not read about the details of fitting ski boots. Jim assured me I was properly fitted, even though I insisted that I wanted the other skis—the ones for the pros. "No, Marsh, first-time skiers need to wear short skis. Trust me," Jim insisted.

We put my nubby little skis inside the van and within minutes were at the ski resort. Again, I was not prepared to pay $30 for a one-day ski pass. Another minor detail had been left out of my handy ski book.

Fees paid, skis in locked position, jackets zipped, and my survival kit snug in my pocket—I was ready. As I waited for Jim and Karen to release their kids for the day, I gazed up the mountain. A sudden pang penetrated my soul and body to the core. *How am I supposed to get up there?* I thought.

Jim tapped me on the shoulder and asked, "Ready for your first lesson?"

"Ready, Coach. But, this should be a snap. First, how do we get up there?" I asked. Jim laughed as he led me to the ski lift.

"You mean we have to ride that up the mountain?" I asked.

"Would you rather climb?" Jim laughed as he led me to the lift. No sooner had we stood in line until the lift swooped us up. It swayed as

Falling Forward

our feet and skis dangled below. Slowly, we climbed the mountain. I could see Karen and the kids waving. Suddenly, I realized they were becoming smaller as we drifted upward.

"Jim, they do stop this thing for us to get off, don't they?" I asked.

Again, Jim only laughed and smiled. At the precise moment, he belted me on the back insisting it was our turn to depart the lift. "We ski off—now!" Jim shouted.

No one was more surprised than I when I realized I was standing. I had not fallen. *This really will be easy*, I thought.

Jim instructed me to go over to the departure area and wait. He needed to adjust his skis. Nothing is as awkward as walking on planks. Yet, I made it.

While waiting, I realized another detail that had been left out of my ski book—waiting. Delicate balance is required to wait on icy snow. One's skis should never be parallel.

I remember learning something about gravity in college physics, and was beginning to understand its effect as my body started sliding down the slope. Within an instant, I was downhill bound, traveling at the rate of gravity's pull—maybe thirty miles an hour. Jim suddenly realized I had gone. He tried to catch up. I was totally out of control but still standing tall on the wooden planks.

Jim was desperate. He screamed, "The woman has never skied before."

Skiers quickly moved to the edge of the ski path to make room for the woman skiing straight down the mountain—gaining momentum with every moment.

"Snowplow!" Jim shouted.

Snowplow? I thought as I gazed from side to side searching for some sort of snow tractor. My book had not mentioned the words *snowplow*. That is ski language for *stop*. Within seconds, I was approaching the bottom of the mountain. My speed was incredible. I was still standing and had two useless poles dragging behind, still in my hands.

Then I saw it—the parking lot. In front of the sea of automobiles and vans was a white wall—the ski wall. It was a ten-foot mound of snow designed for people who did not know how to "snowplow." I had no sooner seen it than I experienced it. My body, two nubby skis, and dangling poles crashed into it with the greatest of speed. My body was so

With Love, Marsha

firmly implanted that it took Jim and another man to pull me out. People were standing around taking pictures of my body's imprint in the snow. The paramedic team arrived to see if my bones were still bones and not mush. Fortunately, nothing was hurt except my pride. I could hear Joni and Alan standing at the foot of the mountain, laughing and shouting, "Way to go, Marsha!"

Father, it was humiliating. I learned that reading a book on skiing is not the answer, and practicing in your room does not help. Learning to ski means having a firsthand experience on the mountain, with equipment in hand and the instructor by your side. Part of the learning process is listening to those who have already learned. Sometimes the most unlikely people can be our teachers—Joni and Alan. Learning means getting up after falling down. It means falling forward.

I did learn to ski before the sun set but not until I had fallen dozens of times. Each fall was harder to recover. I wept with pain as I discovered muscles I did not realize I had. They began to take hold precisely the moment I was willing to let go of my pride and listen to my teacher. It was then that the "ah-ha" moment came—it simply clicked.

The information and the motions finally married. Freedom and joy came in equal proportion to the pain the moment I gained control of the skis. No longer were the skis controlling me. I was controlling them as I kept the rules and continued to concentrate on my instructions. Yet, the moment I focused my attention on anything else, I fell.

Father, my Christian life is so similar. How often have I felt I had nothing else to learn? After all, I had read Your letters. How often have I been too proud to learn from others, simply because I felt superior in one way or other? How often have I felt that practicing in the security of my own private world was good enough? How often have I fallen so frequently that I discovered pain I never knew existed? It is wonderful when I recognize the freedom that is mine when I follow Your rules.

Father, may I always keep my sights on You as my instructor. May I always be eager to learn—not just when I fall, but when I am soaring. When I let every moment and every experience be a teachable moment, I am then sincerely Yours.

With love,
Marsha

The Gift

Dear Child:

Since you are eager to have spiritual gifts, try to excel in gifts that build up the church.

For it is by grace you have been saved, through faith—and this not from yourselves, it is the gift of God—not by works, so that no one can boast.

We have different gifts, according to the grace given us. If a man's gift is prophesying, let him use it in proportion to his faith. If it is serving, let him serve; if it is teaching, let him teach; if it is encouraging, let him encourage; if it is contributing to the needs of others, let him give generously; if it is leadership, let him govern diligently; if it is showing mercy, let him do it cheerfully.

Your Father
(1 Cor. 14:12; Eph. 2:8-9; Rom. 12:6-8)

With Love, Marsha

Dear Father:

Some of my favorite childhood memories are family times. As I read Your letter about gifts, I remembered the family custom we shared each winter watching *The Wizard of Oz*. I remember the thrill and anticipation generated by Dorothy, the Scarecrow, the Tin Man, and the Lion as they escaped various perils in order to meet the Wizard. They were convinced the Wizard could help them find what they lacked. Dorothy wanted to find her way back to Kansas; the Tin Man wanted a heart; the Scarecrow, a brain; and the Lion, courage.

I recently visited my family. Once again, we watched *The Wizard of Oz*. The plot was exactly as I had remembered it. My interpretation, however, was different. Rather than four unique characters seeking to meet a Wizard, I recognized four characters seeking to meet themselves. Each was called to recognize his or her potential. That recognition came only as they acted on what they had already been given. Part of the discovery was just to use what was already theirs.

While their goals were different, they did have something in common. Each had potential. The Tin Man had the potential to show compassion; the Lion, courage; and the Scarecrow, consciousness. They also had Dorothy who risked seeing the obvious in each of them.

The drama intensified as the Emerald City proved not to have what they sought. The Wizard was a fake. As they dwelled in their disappointments, Dorothy was kidnapped. Each was compelled to act quickly; there was no time to focus on self. In an effort to rescue her, the other three stopped looking and started acting. Without hesitating, the Scarecrow used his brain to develop a strategy to save Dorothy. The Tin Man wept with compassion. The Lion courageously made the successful rescue. Together they were a team.

Father, like the characters described, You have gifted me. I am filled with potential, but so often I go looking for something that You have already given me. Already, I am equipped with spiritual gifts. Yet, too often I fail to recognize my gift and exercise my potential. I recognize my gift when I stop looking and start acting.

Challenge me, Father, to hold onto my compassion by using the gifts You have given me to exhibit love. Challenge me to hold onto my consciousness by using my gifts to be aware of opportunities to serve others.

The Gift

Challenge me to hold onto my courage by using my gifts to encourage others to see beyond the obvious. Help me to use my gifts for You.

With love,
Marsha

Out of Sight

Dear Child:

The kingdom of heaven is like a treasure hidden in a field. When a man found it, he hid it again, and then in his joy went and sold all he had and bought that field. Again, the kingdom of heaven is like a merchant looking for fine pearls. When he found one of great value, he went away and sold everything he had and bought it.

Your Father
(Matt. 13:44-46)

Out of Sight

Dear Father:

I did it again. I removed all evidence of the work that had embedded my office. It was not difficult. I merely transferred all unanswered memos, correspondence, and unfinished projects from my "to do" box on the corner of my desk to my "to do" folder under my desk inside a burgundy briefcase. I can walk out of my office knowing my desk is clear. I will, of course, need a wheelbarrow to carry the briefcase.

I must admit that I have the tendency to put things out of sight. By doing so, they are out of mind! It is really not difficult. I just remove from sight all reminders of the oughts and shoulds. I wonder if other people are tempted to play this game. I know when I play it. And, I must acknowledge that I play it in other playing fields, too. I am guilty of putting dried clothes back into the dryer to escape folding them. I have used a closet or an unnoticed corner of a room to collect things I did not know what else to do with. I have stuffed unpaid bills into my small desk drawer to avoid the nagging reminder of my lack of money. Second thought, maybe others do join the ranks of active "out of sight—out of mind" participants.

By removing obvious reminders of what I have not done, I trick myself into believing all is well. I temporarily feel in control of my life. As I remove the constant reminders of things left undone, I likewise remove the guilt of ought and should.

Father, can I be free from this game of hide and seek? Is it procrastination, lack of responsibility, or a common human tendency that has uncommon implications? I know my excuses. I can even name them:

- I don't have time, now.
- I don't know how, yet.
- I must first give my full attention to the urgent.
- It doesn't fit into my plans for today.
- If I don't do it, someone else more qualified will.

Yes, Father, these are excuses, reasons that do not yield results. Instead they have consequences that include not meeting a deadline; permanently wrinkled clothes; or receiving notices from collection agencies, suggesting that I pay attention to the bills stuffed in my desk drawer. But the tragedy is that regardless of the excuse, I know that within me are all the resources for accomplishing each task.

With Love, Marsha

In most cases, this game is harmless. Yet, sometimes it is dangerous. For example, there are those times when I avoid those who are hurting, undesirable, lost, uneducated, and uncultured. It is easier simply to pretend they are not there. Father, like the unpaid bills, I have been guilty of putting them out of sight by removing myself from their presence. Father, this reminds me of my trip to Brazil in 1982. I remember seeing the lost, hungry, hurting, dying, sick, and genuinely helpless. There were thousands of them packed into those five-square-block communities made of cardboard boxes and strips of metal. I remember the feelings of discomfort and the desire to escape. I wanted to hide or pretend that what I was seeing wasn't real. I wanted to be in my comfortable home. I was not prepared to deal with all I saw. But since I could not escape, I was unable to tuck those unpleasant sights inside my "spiritual" drawer. I had to acknowledge what was real. Only then could God use me because part of what was real was within me. Inside of me was the potential to make a contribution to their lives.

Even after that spiritually boggling experience, I have at times fallen back into the tendency to sweep under the rug what I prefer to go unnoticed. How often I have failed you by responding to the hurting by saying, "I do not have the time to minister and witness" or, "I do not feel adequate to do anything about it."

How often I have seen and recognized the importance of responding, yet felt overwhelmed by the urgency of something I had defined as important, that I did not respond? *It does not fit into my schedule nor does it help me to accomplish the items on my "to-do list,"* I have thought.

And yes, I have been guilty of seeing a need and failing to respond because I have been so deeply convinced that someone else more qualified should respond.

Father, Your letter today has challenged me in two ways. First, I need to recognize how I practice "out of sight, out of mind" in the spiritual area of my life. Second, I need to respond by rearranging my priorities so that the urgent does not crowd out the important.

Make my life a priority letter to be sent to those in need. Let's send it first class.

With love,
Marsha

The Resolution

Dear Child:

So we make it our goal to please him, whether we are at home in the body or away from it.

Are you so foolish? After beginning with the Spirit, are you now trying to attain your goal by human effort?

Not that I have already obtained all this, or have already been made perfect, but I press on to take hold of that for which Christ Jesus took hold of me. Brothers, I do not consider myself yet to have taken hold of it. But one thing I do: Forgetting what is behind and straining toward what is ahead, I press on toward the goal to win the prize for which God has called me heavenward in Christ Jesus.

The goal of this command is love, which comes from a pure heart and a good conscience and a sincere faith.

For you are receiving the goal of your faith, the salvation of your souls.

Your Father
(2 Cor. 5:9; Gal. 3:3; Phil. 3:12-14; 1 Tim. 1:5; 1 Pet. 1:9)

With Love, Marsha

Dear Father:

I do it each year. My intentions are always worthy. On January 1, I set resolutions/goals. I write down the things I want to accomplish, habits I wish to break, and standards I wish to maintain. The cycle seems to repeat itself. I do well for a while. But as days yield to months, the spark of my lofty ambitions slowly dwindles into ashes.

What is a goal, Father? Is it worthwhile to set standards? How do I stay on track when so many other noble intentions and ambitions seem to infiltrate my day, causing my goals to be derailed or at least sidetracked in other directions?

I am jolted out of bed by the clock radio at precisely the same time each morning. I eat at the same time. Twice a month I have a predetermined amount of money set aside for savings. Once or twice a month, I complete reading one book on my "haven't read yet" shelf in my study. I have an idea of exactly what I want to weigh. I am committed to walking four miles a day. I spend the first minutes each morning in quiet time in which only coffee, Your presence, and a few good inspirational books are allowed.

What do all of these unrelated life-style mannerisms have in common? In one way or another, they each represent a goal. Where did they come from? Me! I have placed a premium on certain life-style actions. How did they become incorporated into my life-style? Through choice, dedication, conviction, discipline, and practice.

Father, I am no expert in goal management. There are many persons who claim to be. Bookstore shelves are stacked with self-help books on how to set and maintain goals in nearly every area of life. Goal setting ranges from how to pay for your home in five years, start a business, maintain the perfect weight, and keep a spiritual journal.

With such emphasis on goals in our society, I am interested in how goal setting merges with my Christian life-style. In all my research, I have discovered little attention given to setting spiritual goals. I guess I have always thought setting spiritual goals limited the spontaneous actions of Your Holy Spirit in my life.

Your letters have helped me realize that unless my goal is deeply rooted in Your will for my life, it is only my selfish ambition. Such ambition is often covered by religious masks. I want my goals to be

The Resolution

from You. I have realized that only when my goals are set by You can I be empowered to reach them.

Several years ago, I heard the story of a most unlikely winner. It's the story of a young boy first "plagued" with the name Oren. In 1947 San Francisco's Potrero Hill was not only a poor neighborhood, it was a real ghetto. That was the year Oren was born. Rickets, a poverty-related disease caused by malnutrition, was Oren's major problem. His vitamin-mineral-deficient diet caused his bones to soften. His legs began to bow under the weight of his growing body. His family was too poor to afford braces. The result was a pigeon-toed, bowlegged young boy who soon was nicknamed "Pencil Legs."

But something happened to change the direction of Oren's life. He recognized his differences and his limitation. He then refused to let such limitations stand in his way. He was motivated to become somebody that could impact the world.

As an eleven-year-old boy, Oren attended a banquet honoring the legendary NFL running back, Jim Brown. Jim challenged the young ghetto boys to be different. He encouraged them to set goals. After the motivational speech, Oren made his way to the champion and said, "I'll break every record you have ever set."

"You do that," said Jim Brown. Oren did just that. Oren J. Simpson was one of football's greatest. He ran the length of the football field with record speed. He continues to challenge others to set goals. But achieving his goal did not happen overnight for O. J. It took time, practice, persistence, falling down, and the courage to get back up again. Can we as Christians capture this same enthusiasm for setting and achieving goals? We can!

Unlike our physical life in which we are not born equally, spiritually we are all capable of becoming goal achievers. But it will take more than determination and will power to reach spiritual goals. Reaching spiritual goals of becoming all that You have created me to become demands the power found in Your will. Goals are accomplished in my spiritual life through Your perfect timing. The joy of it all is not achieving the goal but running the race.

Father, teach me Your way. What spiritual goals do I need to set? What changes do I need to make and what priorities do I need to rearrange in order to reach Your goals? I am convinced that much of the

With Love, Marsha

joy and satisfaction of goal achieving is the journey. As I proceed toward the goal of Your calling, may my life demonstrate what it means to be Yours.

With love,
Marsha

The Search

Dear Child:
You have searched me and you know me. You know when I sit and when I rise; You perceive my thoughts from afar. You discern my going out and my lying down; You are familiar with all my ways. Before a word is on my tongue You know it completely, O Lord.
Search me, O God, and know my heart; Test me and know my anxious thoughts. See if there is any offensive way in me, And lead me in the way everlasting.

Your Father
(Ps. 139:1-4; 22-24)

With Love, Marsha

Dear Father:

Today was truly a horrible, terrible, very bad, no-good sort of day! Everything that could go wrong did and at the worst possible moment. Any positive encounter with another person was merely coincidental. I felt an alternating rhythm between two extremes as my pendulum swung from survival to sanity.

If confession is good for the soul, consider my soul in good shape. Today nothing felt good, looked good, or even happened that was good.

When this day started, it was the coldest morning of the year. I had an early morning meeting at the office. Normally, I am a morning person; perhaps I stayed up too late last night. Regardless, I overslept. My subconscious must have heard the alarm go off. When I was finally awoke, I found the clock tucked under the cover next to my body in my warm bed. As soon as I realized the time, I jumped up and grabbed the only clean shirt I had starched and ironed. I headed for the shower.

There the already late start became even later. Because of my hurried state, I forgot to properly adjust the water temperature. The moment I jumped in, I scalded my head. Leaping out quickly was not a smart move. I did an incredible slide across the icy cold tile floor. My head hit first.

I quickly convinced myself that I did not have time for head injuries. So, I readjusted the water temperature and started over, this time to be greeted with an eye full of shampoo. As I reached for the towel, I missed. It was my last clean starched shirt. How could I tell it wasn't the towel? After all, both eyes were glued shut.

The shower experience was enough to start anyone's day off with a literal bang! Bad became worse when my left contact lens decided to permanently reside in the sink's drain rather than my eye. There wasn't enough time for breakfast, much less to be with You as I normally am.

Dressed, with one contact lens, a wet shirt, a bruised head, and a wounded spirit, I grabbed my keys, coat, and briefcase and rushed to the car.

Perfect, I thought as I somehow got a run in my stockings from scraping ice from the windshield. *Never mind. I have a meeting in three minutes*, I thought frantically.

My driving speed matched my intensity. So did the voice of the police officer who pulled me over for speeding. How I talked myself out of that

The Search

ticket, I'll never know. Maybe it was the wet shirt and obvious lack of a contact lens that did it. It certainly was not my charming personality. I made it to the office only eight minutes late. When I entered the room where the meeting was to be held, I wondered if I had blown it again. *Where is everyone?* I thought.

The meeting had been canceled! I was not a happy person. I was mad, hungry, hurting, spiritually malfunctioning, and depressed. How I felt was obvious, not only to me but to everyone else. They declared it, "Be-nice-to-Marsha day," punctuating the statement with, "She's a little on edge." I was as sensitive as a spider's web. I seemed to attract all kinds of little creatures.

My inner feelings seemed to show up in everything I did. I felt horrible about myself and about everyone else. No one could live up to my expectations. If I made a significant difference in anyone's life that day, it was certainly coincidental—by chance, not choice.

But I learned something today, Father. When my internal world is in shambles, my external world reflects that state of being. When I feel poorly about who I am, I lack the ability to communicate anything positive about who He is. I am thankful for forgiveness, Father, and for a second chance to learn, grow, and fall forward. I am likewise thankful for you—my Father whose love for me is unconditional.

Where do I go now to continue to receive and nurture Your inner source that provides stamina, positive determination, and the unswerving ability to look consistently at events in a day in a different way? Can I really have spiritual solitude on such stormy days?

I must be open to days like today. I must be open to learn as I find myself in the hub of life's many perplexities. Like the hub of a wheel, the pattern of my day is essentially circular, but I must be open to all points, both good and bad. There must be that balanced tension between retreat and return. Will you, Father, be the hub centering my life? Will you be my retreat in the midst of my storm? Will you balance my days so I can return to the hurting well as one whose sensitivity attracts Your magnificent creation within?

I write from my innermost woven parts. They are Yours.

With love,
Marsha

About the Author

Marsha G. Spradlin is a much sought-after speaker and free-lance writer from Mobile, Alabama. In addition to *With Love, Marsha*, she has authored *Transformed One Winter*, *Livingtouch: Your Personal Witness in an Impersonal World*, *INtouch: Women of Faith in the 90s*, and hundreds of articles.

She previously served with the Woman's Missionary Union of the Southern Baptist Convention and the Baptist General Convention of Texas.

She was educated at the University of South Alabama (B.S.), and Southwestern Baptist Theological Seminary (M.R.E.) and has done postgraduate study at East Texas State University.

For further information you may write her at P.O. Box 180371, Mobile, Alabama 36618 or call her at 205-452-3133.